Faith
and
Understanding
in
America

THE MACMILLAN COMPANY
NEW YORK · CHICAGO
DALLAS · ATLANTA · SAN FRANCISCO
LONDON · MANILA

IN CANADA
BRETT-MACMILLAN LTD.
GALT, ONTARIO

FAITH
AND
UNDERSTANDING
IN
AMERICA

✦✦✦

Gustave Weigel, S.J.

NEW YORK
THE MACMILLAN COMPANY
1959

Imprimi Potest: William F. Maloney, S.J.
                  Praep. Prov.

Nihil Obstat: Edward A. Cerny, S.S.
                  Censor Librorum

Imprimatur: ✠ Francis P. Keough, D.D.
                  Archbishop of Baltimore
                  October 14, 1958

First Printing

Library of Congress catalog card number: 59-5989

The Macmillan Company, New York
Macmillan-Brett Ltd., Galt, Ontario

Printed in the United States of America

FOR PERMISSION to use, generally in revised form, material from previously published essays, grateful acknowledgment is hereby made to the holders of the original copyrights. The previously published essays are:

"The Meaning of the Moment" which appeared in *Cross Currents* (II, 3, p. 56); "Ecumenism and the Catholic" which was originally printed in *Thought* (XXX, 116, p. 248), published in 1955 by Fordham University Press; "Protestant Theological Positions Today" and "Protestantism as a Catholic Concern" which were published in separate issues of *Theological Studies* (XI, 4, p. 62; XVI, 2, p. 38), in 1950 and 1955 by Theological Studies, Inc.; "Catholic and Protestant Theologies in Outline" which appeared in *The American Scholar* (XXV, 3, p. 289), published in 1956 by the United Chapters of Phi Beta Kappa; and "An Introduction to American Catholicism," a Chapter of THE CATHOLIC CHURCH, U.S.A., edited by Louis J. Putz, C.S.C., published by Fides Publishers Association, in 1956 by Fides Publishers Association, Chicago, Ill.

Preface

THE TOPICS discussed in this volume, while they may appear diverse from certain points of view, are essentially one in relation to the general problem of faith and world order in current society. To this larger problem I have addressed myself on numerous occasions in recent years. It is my hope that this collection of my essays and lectures will prove of interest and help to those seeking to unravel the difficulties of faith against the backdrop of modern history.

In gathering the various essays and lectures which compose this book, I have received the encouragement of many friends and students. My former student, Mr. Thomas P. Coffey, was most helpful in reworking the various essays and in suggesting the order in which they should appear. Father Walter J. Ong, S.J., has kindly proposed a title for the volume. To all these friends, advisers, and collaborators I wish to express my heartfelt thanks.

Gustave Weigel, S.J.

Contents

Faith
and
Understanding
in
America

I

✢✢✢

The Catholic Conception of
Religious Truth

✢✢✢

FAITH HAS different meanings for a Catholic and a Protestant. To the Protestant, faith means a trusting self-surrender of the complete man to the revealing God. For a Catholic, however, this act of cordial surrender is called faith, hope, and charity. To a Catholic, the word "faith" conveys the notion of an intellectual assent to the content of revelation as true because of the witnessing authority of God the Revealer.

Consequently the Catholic understands faith intellectually and supernaturally. Faith is the Catholic's response to an intellectual message communicated by God. For the Catholic, God reveals Himself through the medium of the teaching of the living holy community called the Church. It is so important for non-Catholics to appreciate this from the outset. A Christian of the Reform tradition believes that God makes Himself and His truth known through a collection of books called the Bible. This book is the teacher, and all other teaching is commentary, good or bad. The divine message itself is restricted to the Book.

In the light of these basic observations we can see the great difference between the Catholic and Protestant conceptions of the God-encounter. For the Catholic, the locus of meeting is the Church, which for its task of bringing men to God uses many means: the teaching of authorized masters, that is, the bishops and their primate the Pope; the liturgy; books written by men of the Church under divine inspiration, the Scriptures; the common beliefs and practices of the Catholics stretched out over time and space. The inspired books, which have God as their author in consequence of their inspiration, are ecclesiastical instruments for teaching, guiding and exhorting. They are not over the Church, but rather a part of the Church's panoply to be used in her work of accomplishing the task of uniting man to God. It is the Church which teaches, the Church which sanctifies, the Church which builds and vitalizes. The Church is not a fruit of the Book but rather the Book is a fruit of the Church.

Hence it is that the Catholic does not say in the first instance, What does the Book say? Rather he asks, What does the teaching Church say? The Church and the Book say the same thing, and since the Book is in a peculiar sense God's Word, he will turn to the Book. However, this is not his ultimate recourse. He has only one ultimate recourse, the Church herself, and the Book is accepted from her hand and with her explanation. The Book is not the proof but only a divine expression in human language of the Church's teaching. Over the Book stands the Church, while according to the Reform conception, over the Church stands the Book.

This fundamental vision of the Church causes the Catholic to look to the episcopate for doctrine, because the bishops are the authentic exponents of God's message to the world. This is no idolatry of the bishops or their primate, the Bishop of Rome, but only a consequent of the Catholic theory of the Church. The Church is an organized visible fellowship theologically explained by the great scriptural symbols of the People of God, the Vine and Branches, the Body of Christ, the Temple of the Holy Ghost, the Marriage of Christ and his Spouse. Because it is a visible society, it has the social structure of such a union. Because it is divine in institution and dynamism, the Holy Spirit dwells in it, keeping it alive, keeping it true, making it grow. The Spirit is the source of the life of the Church, but that life is the life of a body. The body is made up of many members which are distinguished one from the other by functions for which they have a fixed structure. The hand is not the foot nor is the eye the ear, though all are in the Body and all live the one life of the Body. (I Corinthians 12.)

In the Body, the bishops have the function of teaching and guiding, and this task they perform through the power of the Spirit who transfuses the whole Body, making each member effective in his function. The Body is one, and so the episcopate is one, as St. Cyprian said seventeen centuries ago. The unity of the episcopate is achieved through solidarity with the prime source of episcopal power, the Bishop of Rome, who is the successor of Simon changed into the Rock, on whom the Church was built and who received the keys of the Kingdom. In the primate dwells the fullness of episcopal power, and all bishops share it with him. Altogether they have no more than he has and he alone has all that they have.

Therefore, the Catholic sees in the Bishop of Rome the supreme source of teaching and guidance. In that man the episcopate is fully gathered; by means of the episcopate the Church teaches; through the indwelling power of the Holy Spirit the Church teaches because with the Spirit as the soul and the believers as the members, one living Body is formed and it is the Body of Christ Himself, God's definitive legate to the world for redemption, sanctification and doctrine.

So it is that in the Catholic vision the Pope teaches in the name of the episcopate and the episcopate teaches in the name of the Church and the Church teaches in the name of Christ, and Christ teaches in the name of God.

The above describes Catholic theory in blueprint fashion. It is the basic two-dimensional outline of a three-dimensional reality. In life the outline will lose its angularity, take on curves, deviate pleasingly from the rectilinear projection. In the hurly-burly of historical existence the severe fundamental outlines may not be noticed at first glance, and it will take much study to see them. This the Catholic knows as well as the non-Catholic. As a result one of the most important and most difficult tasks of the Catholic theologian is to keep in view the fundamental figure. To do so he will have to distinguish between the curves added by history to the plan established by God. The curves must be there, for otherwise it would not be a portrait of a historical thing. But the curves do not distort the basic lines; they only make them historically alive.

In consequence, the reading of the papal message over two millennia can give a historian a good index of the problems which vexed men in the Church in her contact with history. All of the pronouncements had some historical stimulus. In a period of perfect calm where there is no attacking storm, the Popes do not speak, for there is no necessity. The struggles of the Christian in the concrete *mise en scène* of his moment call for guidance and light, and since it is the function of the episcopate to supply them, the Popes will never fail to teach if the problems are more than local. The center of the episcopate will give the Christian message for the total Church.

Hence there is always a historical factor in papal teaching. The Pope speaks for a definite moment of time, though he communicates a transhistorical message. The very language and forms of encyclicals show historical influences. The style is the so-called "curial style," set ages ago according to the norms of Roman rhetoric, for the papal language is usually Latin. This style is quite different from that of the vernaculars employed today, but the stability of the style is an eloquent witness to the Church's temporal continuity. The formalized style often succumbs to current needs: words like "typewriter," "motorcycle" and "aeroplane," for which the Romans had no counterpart, must be invented. That the communications are in Latin is because of the historical fact that the papacy is rooted in the ancient city of Rome with its language and style. That we see modern, invented words is because of the fact that the pronouncement deals with a contemporary situation.

When dealing with a contingent set of circumstances a question which seems merely abstract actually takes on very concrete meaning, and the total question is not a purely speculative one. Existentialist factors predominate. Into such a setting a question and its answer have burning facets which are far removed from abstract neutrality.

An analogy will serve to explain the point. Desegregation is an unemotional word in itself. In the light of such principles as the Christian brotherhood of man or Jacobin egalitarianism, the reality expressed by the word would be unassailable. Even in environments where the notion is not consciously related to principles, the label is not a fighting word. It may have this neutral quality in a place like Helsinki, Finland, but the situation in Biloxi, Mississippi, is altogether different. For Biloxians, something more than the simultaneous presence of Negro and white children in the same school is understood. In the minds of Southerners segregation is only one factor in a constellation of meaning, and an attack on the single factor is considered to be an attack on the total constellation. Segregation and desegregation have concrete meaning because of concrete circumstances.

I doubt strenuously if even the abstract question of desegregation could have arisen in Finland.

Consequently papal directives face not only abstract problems but emotionally loaded concrete human situations. The hierarch must at one and the same time function as teacher and as director of communal coexistence. The direction is clearly for a concrete set of circumstances which will change with the movement of time. The doctrine is atemporal and always valid. Yet to divide the passing elements from the stable substance is not so easy.

Even an abstract proposition can produce communal nervousness by the very fact that its expression is an event in a community. The meaning of the abstract formula and its relevancy to the world vision of the group where the formula was launched may not be clear at a given moment, but the presence of the formula with all the acrid debates it arouses may be disturbing practically. The wise chairman of the meeting will shelve such a question and adroitly close the debate. The question is not answered because it seems inopportune to examine it in a heated environment. The question is not closed; only the debate.

Much of papal instruction shows this directional concern of the Popes. They deal not only with speculative theory but with the very practical repercussions of such theory in a given community at a given time. Thus conflicting teaching seems to be given by the same or successive Popes. It is easy to find papal affirmations in condemnation of democracy as well as papal praise of democracy. It is not wise to say that we have here a reversal of position. It is equally unwise to use one set of statements as indicative of the papal policy without referring to the other set. Jacobin antireligious democracy was certainly condemned, but American democracy has been frequently lauded. Democracy is a chameleon word. The Soviet conception of democracy is not what the British understand by the term, and Mussolini said that fascism was the most democratic society of all. When the Pope speaks, he therefore must bear in mind to whom he is speaking and what the words can mean for his audience. The caution of papal communications can be seen in the subtitle of Pius XI's *Divini redemptoris* (1937), in which orthodox Marxist communism is rejected. The subtitle is: *On* atheistic *communism*. Whether or not a communism can be constructed in accord with Christian revelation is not being discussed. For many a student of the encyclicals, especially those in whom zeal outruns discretion, the cautious modifiers introduced into papal propositions are annoying. However, the Popes realize full well the responsibility of their office, and they are always aware that after them there will come other Popes who must not be embarrassed by previous solutions of concrete problems. The Popes word their doctrine with extreme precision for a definite historical context, so that the doctrine will not necessarily take on meanings beyond those needed for the question to be treated here and now.

This qualification of papal communications, if overlooked, can lead to what the Germans call *Konsequenzmacherei*. The word means that conclusions are drawn out of given propositions with the aid of premises which the individual believes in, but which are not necessarily admitted by the original author of the propositions. The result will be that doctrine is attributed to the Popes which they not only did not teach but which they reject. An example of this kind of procedure can be shown in the following form of reasoning which has often been foisted on the public. "The Popes are opposed to Marxist communism. But Marxist communism is the betterment of the lot of the workers. Therefore the Popes are opposed to the betterment of the lot of the workers." This is a mischievous presentation of papal doctrine. The Popes have made it very clear over and over again that they seek the betterment of the situation of the workers. They have declared without ceasing that this is one of the principal Christian tasks of our time. What they deny is that atheistic communism is the amelioration of the workingman's condition. To interpret the Popes in the light of premises which they expressly repudiate is hardly an honest interpretation of their teaching.

At times Catholics themselves fall into the same trap. By projecting the papal message, they produce statements which are not the affirmations of the Popes but which seem to the interpreters logically inevitable conclusions. However, the logic operates by the force of tacit or even unconscious assumptions which are not at all shared by the authors of the encyclicals. The interpreters then in bludgeon fashion brandish such extensions as valid papal teaching to beat down opponents who do not understand the Roman doctrine their way.

Another element in Catholic theory must always be borne in mind. It is what Cardinal Newman called the development of doctrine and others call the evolution of dogma. Catholicism insists that it teaches the preaching of Christ and only that. The Catholic believes that his beliefs are identical with those of the Apostolic Church, without a jot or tittle changed. However, he knows that the syntheses made in an earlier day are shorter and more meager than the syntheses made now. The affirmations of the Council of Nicaea (A.D. 325) are fuller affirmations concerning the constitutional structure of Jesus than the original New Testament statements. However, the Catholic insists that the doctrine of Nicaea is the identical doctrine of the New Testament. Nicaea detailed formally and clearly what was implicit in the scriptural formulas. According to Nicaea the scriptural title of Jesus, Christ the Lord, means and always meant that Jesus was God of God, Light of Light, true God of true God. The older phrase did not say it explicitly, but that is what is meant, and Nicaea made the implication explicit. The manner in which such explicitness is realized is generically the same in all ages. The serene faith of the total Church becomes agitated by some theologian who declares that the old and accepted formulas mean thus and so. When the theologian interprets the perennial expressions counter to the living consciousness of the Church, the *magisterium,* that is, the teaching authorities, will reformulate the old expression so that the innovator's interpretations will be excluded. The new expression is obviously longer than the old one, but it is not a different one.

The way of development must be correctly understood. The drawing out of the implications from the older formula is not done mainly—much less exclusively—by a philological method. We can explain the philological method superficially by the example of the classical response of the oracle when asked by Pyrrhus if he could defeat the Romans: you will come out of the battle with the Romans victorious. The proposition is ambiguous. It can mean that the Romans will be victorious and it can just as readily mean that Pyrrhus will be the victor. It all depends on which word "victorious" modifies. Does it modify "Romans" or does it modify "you"? We cannot tell by mere literary analysis which meaning we are to take out of the statement. Two entirely different programs can be built for the guidance of Pyrrhus, and the builders of the different programs will quarrel among themselves, each insisting that he has the proper understanding of the prophecy. They must, however, ultimately use some principle of interpretation other than mere linguistic analysis. This other principle will then decide how we are to render the ambiguous answer of the oracle. The easiest solution would be to ask the oracle what she meant, but in the case of Pyrrhus this tactic was pointless, because the oracle on principle did not know what was meant. She repeated what the god inspired her to say. She was as much in the dark as Pyrrhus.

Yet in Catholic theory this easy solution is possible. The doctrine of Christ *lives* in the Catholic Church. At any moment, because of the abiding indwelling Spirit of God, the doctrine is known by the total Church, just as a man knows his total knowledge. If you quote to such a man a phrase he used on a former occasion, he can tell you what he meant by it and what he did not mean by it. If you argue with him that the words by linguistic analysis mean the opposite of what he is now saying, he will tell you that you misunderstand the meaning of the former phrase. This may not sound convincing to you, but the man is actually the only one who knows what he meant. He does not at all feel bound to understand his mind by your literary analysis of his words, because he knows what the words meant, even if it is not the meaning you derive from them. He may even explain to you why he used the particular words of his original statement by pointing to the concrete circumstances in which he was then talking, and he refuses to have you tear those words from their original context, which was a context of historical circumstances and not a mere context of words. There is a fluidity in verbal expression, because language is not a system of mathematical symbols with one and only one meaning attached to them.

The development of doctrine is the growth in awareness of the total content carried by ancient formulas. The result of such increased awareness will be new expression of old doctrine in the light of the impact of historical forces. The doctrine is the same but deeper and wider levels of its meaning are grasped and expressed.

The development of doctrine is a question of growth—the growth of the whole Church. The magisterium does not alone produce this development; it only formalizes it in due time. The episcopate with its center in Rome rejects invalid development and incorporates genuine reality into its teachings. The development, like all growth, is slow, almost imperceptible in short periods of time. The whole Church is involved in the process, for it is in the whole Church that the Spirit works. The first manifestations of growth will be in the meditations of the Church's theologians. They will formulate, often quite unconsciously, the living expansion. The theologians do not make the doctrine; they find it. The formulations of the theologians are not the authentic expression of the Church's teaching; only the magisterium can authentically express it. But the theologians are commissioned for their task by the directing magisterium and they work under its constant vigilance. They do more than merely repeat the authentic declarations; they compare them with the other sources of doctrine; they systematize their findings; they talk the language of their time and are very much under the influence of history. Hence it is that the consensus of the Church's theologians actually is the true echo of the teaching Church, for in the theologians we have the amplification of the authentic message so that it can be heard effectively by audiences gathered in many points of the ecumenical Church. Until the consensus is reached, there will be wranglings among the theologians and the famous *odium theologicum* will raise its ugly head, but time as the instrument of the Holy Spirit will bring about gradually and quietly the consensus which the magisterium will canonize when there is need to do so.

It is a matter of great importance for all to understand the difference between the Catholic and non-Catholic conceptions of religious truth. The Reformers of the sixteenth century had as their intention the restoration of the genuine religious life of the early Apostolic Church. Actually this project was not restricted to the followers of Luther and

Calvin. It was the goal of a great number of Catholics as well, and these men finally realized their ambition in the Council of Trent (1545–1563). What distinguished the Catholic reformers from the Protestants was their method. The Protestants thought that they had a way of knowing the doctrines and practices of the Apostolic Church without recourse to the Church's magisterium. They felt that the Scriptures without the episcopate could give any reader the portrait of the true Church and its doctrine. They had, therefore, recourse to philosophy and literary analysis. They also believed that the Spirit would enlighten the reading, not so much through His presence in the total Church but through His immediate action on the reader.

Consequently it is part of the Protestant tradition to suspend judgment on doctrine until the individual is satisfied that he can find it in the Scriptures, for "the whole counsel of God, concerning all things necessary for his own glory, man's salvation, faith and life is either expressly set down in Scripture, or by good and necessary consequence may be deduced from Scripture." (*Westminster Confession*, Ch. 1, s. 6. 1647.) Hence it is that most Protestant Christians "test" all religious doctrine by the Bible. No religious teacher, not even the Church, deserves credence unless he teaches what the reader, enlightened by the Spirit, finds in the Scriptures. With the passing of centuries, Protestants do not understand the Scriptures so literally or subtly as their forefathers did, but the principle of personal judgment on religious doctrine is still proper to the Protestant religion. Such personal judgment is, of course, largely determined by the tradition of the community to which the believer belongs. However, the principle is honored in all forms of Protestantism.

Consistently, therefore, the Protestant believer must see for himself that this or that doctrine is true. Before he accepts it, he weighs the doctrine in the balance of his own experience, of his own understanding of the Scriptures, of his own postulates concerning what God should be and say.

This is just the reverse of the Catholic's approach to belief. As the Catholic sees it, he must accept God on God's terms and not his own. It is not for him to "judge" the divine message but only to receive it. Since he receives it from a living teaching organ, he does not have to puzzle over the meaning of the revelation because the ever-present living magisterium can tell him exactly what the doctrine intends. The Catholic will be faced with the problem of reconciling one phase of the teaching with another, but that is essentially a theological enterprise which most people ignore. Theology, after all, is the pursuit of relatively few men.

If non-Catholics will bear this in mind, they will not be puzzled by the docility of the Catholic when he is given religious doctrine. The non-Catholic is so accustomed to work out his religious theory by his own efforts and convictions that it seems strange that the Catholics show no signs of doing what to him is the main task to be done. The basic difference between the Catholic and non-Catholic approach to religious truth is that the non-Catholic *constructs* it in the light of his own experience and needs, while the Catholic *receives* it so that no reconstruction is called for or even in place. Both positions have their logic, but it is well to understand the logic of the Catholic position when confronted with Catholic pronouncements, for otherwise the Catholic position will not be understood. A non-Catholic will probably not like the Catholic way of achieving God's truth, but he should understand that way in order to deal with it intelligently.

2

✦✦✦

The Meaning of the
Historical Moment

✦✦✦

It will be wise to explain the terms of the title before we do anything else. This will also be useful, for it will manifest the task that we have set up and so put us in a position to tackle it intelligently.

We must define the word "meaning." This term is treacherous, because it seems so obvious but when we try to explain its import, we feel quite inadequate. It is like the word "time." For as St. Augustine said, if you do not ask me what it means, I know; but if you ask me, I do not.

Meaning is a correlative to understanding. Now understanding can be opposed to mere experience. We have all experienced a television apparatus, for we have seen the pictures that are produced by such a machine. However, we do not understand it. We cannot make one, nor can we grasp the theories involved in the organization of the mechanism. When we understand the inner workings and the theory, we have grasped the meaning. When we experience, we only establish contact with an object. The man who made the plans for the first television, obviously never saw one, but he understood a television set, and because he understood, he could make one. To understand I must grasp the sheerly intelligible element of a reality. This element makes the reality luminous to the thinking subject. Because of such a grasp he can answer the child's question "what" and "why." Much has been written on the nature of meaning, and it would hardly be to our purpose to go into that question, though I personally follow Plato's doctrine on the subject. Let it suffice to say that meaning is the answer to the question "what" and "why." The child is so dedicated to these two words that he annoys his elders by using them *ad nauseam,* but the child in this matter shows himself to be human. Our difficulties with the "New Art" arise because we do not know what it means, and we feel hopelessly confused by some of the spokesmen of the new movement who tell us that it does not mean anything. We cannot tolerate that reply, because we spontaneously believe that all things must have meaning. If the thing is static or statically considered we ask "what is it" and if the thing is in flux, we ask "why is it moving?" Meaning therefore is the answer to the eternal questions, what and why.

Moment is an easier word to face. It only means, now. However, in this discussion we are considering the now as an element in a larger global period. The now cannot be understood without investigating its roots and flower. Our moment therefore includes all the years from 1918 to some date as yet not discernible.

In the light of these explanations we can say that our discussion wishes to convey an intelligible grasp of the historical period which is pointed for us by 1959. Let us get down to our task.

It is my contention that our moment began in 1918. Such

a contention implies that a historical period ended at the same time. History is continuous; there are no gaps in it. We can distinguish parts but the parts touch and the new part flows from the old without any interruption of the historical process. Out of 1918 rose our moment and to understand it even as different we must understand the color of the moment which ushered in our own.

The year 1918 ended the First World War which began in 1914. The human situation before 1914 was marked with something like stability. Those of us who lived in that time still think of it as a period of calm, repose and order. So much was this the case, that the slogan for the Harding presidential campaign of 1920 was: "Back to normalcy." The unquestioned order of the period before 1914 seemed to the men of the '20's natural and normal, because it was seemingly stable. What were its characteristics?

In order to make living together secure, the late nineteenth century, which historically would include the first thirteen years of the new century, grouped men into three classes. This grouping was set and there was little flux from one class to another. The top class we can call aristocracy, for they considered themselves to be the best and they were commonly called "the betters." This class, numerically very slight in comparison with the totality of mankind, had first call on the good things which the earth produces. They were well fed, sometimes too well fed as the prevalence of gout in those days showed. They were well clad with the best apparel that men could devise in terms of art and utility. They were well housed in mansions conspicuous for their amplitude, elegance and comfort as far as the technological competence of the time allowed. They were served in their human needs, so that they had leisure aplenty. The best of mankind's thought and creation was at their disposal. They read the world's best literature at school and at home. They hung the world's finest pictures in their salons. They held high discourse in their drawing rooms. They also directed the destinies of their communities.

How did one get into this privileged group? Some by birth, though others could enter because of success in acquiring wealth, for the real basis of membership was the possession of wealth. There were two sectors of the group. One sector in terms of inheritance possessed family land, much of it. Their titles to this land were also titles of nobility, and so they were nobles. The land was tilled by others, but the best part of the produce went to the owner and his family, which included "his sisters, his cousins and his aunts." The other sector drew its wealth from industry. They were the industrial and commercial tycoons. The nobles considered them somewhat inferior because their wealth was relatively new, but wealth was power and the industrialists were more numerous and really more powerful, because they controlled more wealth. In the pageantry of tradition they were not so conspicuous, but in the council chambers of government their voices were more penetrating.

Below this class there was another. We call them the bourgeoisie or middle class. As far as secular goods were concerned, they had their share, though it was not excessive. Their food was adequate; their clothes good; their contact with the thought and art of humanity sufficient. However, they had no excess of wealth and they could only make ends meet, and at times this was not too easy. They did not control the destinies of their communities, but they had a conspicuous part and they raised their voices, often enough shrilly. Numerically they were about a fourth of the total community, and they were growing in number.

What were the signs of membership in this class? They were all suppliers of socially needed goods which demanded special training or talent in the supplier: professional men like doctors and lawyers, engineers and architects; clergymen of the diverse religions of the community; teachers and professors of the youth of society; artists in language, music, mass and form; bureaucratic masters of organizational techniques in politics, production or distribution; the foremen of the laboring class. Their goods were scarcer because their numbers were relatively fewer, and on the market place their product was in consequence more precious.

At the bottom of the scale was the proletariat. It was the most numerous class of all, counting about seven tenths of the earth's population. These enjoyed but little of the earth's goods. Their food at best was adequate and at worst deficient. Their clothes in quality and workmanship were poor, except for the colorful costumes of rural traditions, worn rarely and handed down from father to son. The worker's house was mean in the cities and if less mean for the small agricultural landowner, not more comfortable. Leisure was not abundant for this class, and they imbibed little of the learned lore of the ages, for they could not afford long schooling and the development of taste for deeper reading. In Western Europe and North America the vast majority had acquired the skills of reading, writing and calculating, but in Eastern Europe and the Colonial lands the vast majority did not progress as far. Yet this proletariat conserved better than the other classes the *mores* of the past, and as a rule the *Weltanschauung* of an earlier time was languidly conserved in this group. In the direction of the life of the community, their contribution was slight. In the West they could exercise the right of the ballot, but their votes were managed so that they had but little true initiative in making policies, domestic or foreign.

This proletariat was divided into two sections. The western proletariat of Europe and North America precariously occupied a more decent level of living. However, the more numerous proletariat of Asia, Africa and Latin America were in a position that dangerously approached the sub-human. In times of calamity, drought, pest and famine, they slipped below the level. The situation of the colonial worker was worse than that of his fellows in the West because his economy was dependent on, and exploited by, occidental entrepreneurs. They could only produce raw materials for the western consumers and manufacturers. There was little opportunity to elaborate locally the wealth natural to their regions.

The necessity of belonging to this class was hereditary. If the parents had neither wealth nor the capacity to produce an article of higher value for the world's community, the children in turn could only offer their undifferentiated physical energies to the economic functioning of society. For such a contribution the return was never very high, and over vast stretches of the world where such energies abounded, the return was only sufficient for sustenance. The Americas were a source of hope for the European proletariat. The necessity of building up the new continent and the abundant wealth of a thinly populated area gave to the worker a much richer return for his contribution than in crowded Europe, which was already structured and fixedly divided. In consequence, waves of European workers migrated to Canada, the United States and Latin America.

What constituted the proletarian? The employment of the breadwinner of the family group. They were the tillers of the soil, either in small plots owned or rented by the family, or by hiring their services to landowners. They worked in the factories and in the enterprises of transportation. They were the little artisans, shopkeepers and their help. They served the aristocrats as domestic servants or the government in those tasks that required little training and no specialized skills. They performed the humbler services to the community in the creation and maintenance of order, sanitation and public utilities.

These three classes lived side by side, dependent on each other. They were united into national communities functioning civilly through parliamentary organisms which in theory represented the whole people. As a matter of fact, the machine of government was controlled by a clique subject to the veto and often enough to the initiatives of the aristocrats. To ensure the cohesion of the three classes into a communal solidarity, governments tended to control ever larger areas of the lives of the individual citizens and of the citizen groups. In the Americas and England, this tendency was resisted, but in Europe and in the lands imperialistically or economically controlled by Europe the tendency was increasingly effective.

This was the paradox of the moment before ours; it was simultaneously centrifugal and centripetal. Class divisions made for the loosening of the tie that bound all men to the same community, but the government acted effectively to bind all members together by trying to regulate factors of community life where the classes by themselves would only tend to separate one from the other. In any individual community the government was the agency which produced a balance of power in favor of the stability of the *status quo* and in the international community the same tactic was pursued by one great power—Great Britain. There were many other powers, each anxious to expand. The four great powers were Britain, with its mastery of the sea and commerce, the two Germanies which included the stronger German Reich and the precarious Austro-Hungarian union of different nations, France and Russia. There were minor powers in Europe; ailing Turkey, Italy, Spain and the Scandinavian countries.

ᴏment is not yet institutionalized and the existing religious ꜱtitutions are considered by many as colossal fossils, relics the past when they were alive.

In 1914 there were many religious institutions in the ᴡorld. The East was still following the patterns set ages ago, ᴜt the idea of mystical renunciation at the heart of those ᴘatterns was rediscovered by few men, and in one man, Maᴧatma Gandhi, renunciation was being studied and practiced ᴎ order to make it acquisitive by ricochet. In the languid ᴛurkish empire of the Middle East, Islam was active like a ᴢombi. In the West, Christianity was the generic form of institutionalized religion and it took on three forms. The Russian world was Orthodox, but Orthodoxy was an institution completely controlled and employed by the Russian government. There were still saints among the monks but superstition was heavily mixed with the religion of the people, as that strange figure, Rasputin, showed. In the nordic world Protestantism in one form or other took care of the spiritual needs of the people, but the Protestant theologians addicted to liberalism and modernism had washed out of Christianity all that was characteristic and proper to it. Catholicism had a vast diaspora spread all over the world, but its consolidated strength was in the Latin lands. In these lands it was subjected to attack by thinkers and rulers simultaneously, and its influence on society was very weak, so weak that it gave its adversaries the feeling that it was a dying thing. No historic religion was decisive anywhere.

The nascent religion that was working in government, in the universities and on the streets was an optimistic positivistic humanism which we now call "scientist naturalism." (In parenthesis let me say that this is not the same as science, a very innocent thing, but rather a transcendental philosophy parasitically attaching itself to the evident successes of

There was too a growing imponderable a[
United States, fiercely isolationist in its outl[
potential strength. To prevent the expansi[
with the consequent suppression of another[
threw its weight against the challenger, maki[
too dangerous for any one. Britain could do t[
had no intention of expanding. Her colonial e[
enough, vaster than anything that had yet be[
history. Her dominion included Canada which[
she had footholds in Latin America; she co[
Asiatic world through her possession of India a[
parts of lower Africa were hers; while Egypt a[
ranean Africa were subject communities. The on[
to stability was the growing power of Germany[
commerce and military strength, but the relatio[
Britain and Germany were excellent, and in man[
were natural allies.

Nothing would be falser than to suppose that h[
ments can be explained merely by the material f[
tained in them. Wealth and power drives are the en[
make men and communities move, but they themse[
direction. Sheer pursuit of wealth and sheer pursuit[
produce chaos by dissolving society as a human confi[
Ideas restrain and canalize the lusts of men. The[
before ours had its dynamic ideas, and without them[
not understand the moment that posthumously broug[
ours. The basic idea-synthesis of any group or age con[
the religion of that period. However, religions, thou[
marily ideas, yet are also institutions. Often enough re[
institutions outlast their generating idea. When this ha[
the institution is still around, and may have an impr[
and palpable presence, but its dynamic power, the idea,[
longer functioning in society. The typical religion o[

science.) In terms of politics it was called liberalism. This new metaphysics produced a morality and a *Weltanschauung*. If Christianity can be briefly described in the words of Christ (Matthew 6:33): "Seek ye first the kingdom of God and his righteousness and all these things shall be added on to you," then scientistic naturalism could be described as: "Seek ye first the kingdom of man and secular well being, and all things will come eventually." The basic belief was that this earth could be changed into a real paradise, where all the desires of man could be satisfied perfectly. The means to do it were science and its derivative, technology. The sufficiency and inexhaustible potency of visible nature were taken for granted. Equally taken for granted was a push in reality whereby it was always working upward to a happier arrangement of things, and consequently progress was written in the marrow of being, and the longer that humanity would exist, the better it would get. Poverty, disease and ignorance would disappear thanks to science and natural evolution. All that was needed was time. The rich man need not do anything, because all men would reach his condition with the advances of science and technology. The poor man need not revolt, because soon he too would have plenty of the good things of earth. For the moment, only one thing had to be pushed: positivistic science. If in the old Protestant days man was saved by faith alone, in 1912 man was to be saved by science alone. If in the older times government fostered and protected religion, now government fostered and protected science. The reverence that once went to the clergy now went to the workers in the laboratory and to the practitioners of the theories there worked out.

In this scheme of things God was not important. For the perfect adepts of the new vision, there was no other God than the omnipotent powers of nature, which had created heaven and earth, and which had saved man by becoming human through science. The more timid devotees of the new faith did not dare to go that far and still kept a belief in God, but He was pale, veiled and distant. His voice should not be heard and His role was to stimulate men to be more human, for in being truly human they would be divine. Liberal theology had deprived Christ of His divinity and God of His transcendence.

There was a paradoxical phenomenon contemporaneous with this religious creed. There was a little heretical sect which enthusiastically accepted the basic doctrines of the prevailing philosophy, but which believed that the optimistic push in history demanded a revolution to end the nationalist class system, and that it was the function of all good men and true to bring about this event, and they certainly would because it was inevitable in the drives native to history. This sect was called Marxist socialism, or just plain socialism. Needless to say, the aristocrats did not care for this eccentric form of the "true faith," and most of the middle class looked on it with displeasure, though some of the middle class considered it with longing eyes, and the more daring souls joined this little nonconformist chapel.

In the ranks of the proletariat the new faith was not formally accepted. The older religious norms for human behavior were still recognized as valid. However, the worker's adhesion to the religious institutions at hand was not too firm. A small sector actually went over to the Marxist heretical form of secularism, deliberately and knowingly. Another small sector retained an ardent faith in and devotion to the religions of their fathers. Yet the middle mass would do neither. The workers lived together in greater numbers and in closer proximity. The norms of behavior were still the ancient norms, and it was difficult for a member of such a neighborhood to flaunt these norms, because the community would ostracize him. Yet the vision of the churches was no longer vibrant in the class. Life had been secularized and the search for material well-being was universal, with little account made for the Kingdom of God and its justice. The proletariat did not as a whole jettison its traditional religion, but it did relegate it to a subordinate role in life, which of course is a practical rejection, for religion must come first by its own logic, and to give it a secondary place is equivalent to denying it.

Naturalism by itself alone would be a weak religion. It promises only an inevitable heaven. It has no hell and no purgatory. It knows no cross and it will have no dark night of the soul. It does not impel men to sacrifice and renunciation; quite the contrary. It can palliate suffering by considering it the birthpain of a brighter posterity, but men at large feel no love for posterity, least of all a posterity which merely replaces them after they have gone down into nothing. Man needs a transcendental love object, which he can meet here and now. The individualism of the age produced only one such object, the collective ego which was the nation. Nationalism was the romantic element of the vision of the moment that preceded ours. Naturalism was not joyfully accepted, and in its acceptance there were varying degrees of adhesion, but nationalism was fervently universal. Aristocrat and peasant loved their nation. Atheist and orthodox loved the fatherland. Like true romantic love, it was uncritical. An American had phrased it well: "Our country! In her intercourse with foreign nations may she always be in the right; but our country, right or wrong." Nationalism was ambitious, selfish and overweening. It considered every other nation a rival and a possible foe. Almost every nation was looking for expansion and colonial possessions. The flag and the army were always sure of an enthusiastic reception, for did not our banners make tyrannies (that is, other nations) tremble, and were not the army and the navy forever?

It was a strange religion. It had two contradictory elements: naturalism, which had killed gods, and nationalism which had created a new one to the image and likeness of local man.

Nationalism, without which naturalism could not live at all, was dynamite. An inadvertent jolt can make it calamitously explosive. Such an inadvertence took place in 1914. The national power systems, seemingly in equilibrium, clashed for four years. The quarrel was a consuming one, for scientific technology used great quantities of the limited stockpile of physical energy at the disposal of the combatants. However, the opponents could not defeat each other, and they reached a stalemate in utter exhaustion. The war settled no major issues but it did destroy much more than the people of 1918 appreciated. Russia collapsed in structure, and the pieces were being put together in a new pattern, the pattern of the Marxist heresy. Turkey ceased to be of importance. Germany was paralyzed. Britain and France were impoverished. A new great power emerged, the United States of America. Its great wealth had been left intact, for the costs of the war were not beyond its means. Yet there was an aloofness on the part of America, which by tradition feared any entanglements with Europe.

The destruction and suffering caused by the war were without equal in the history of man prior to the event. The armies were quantitatively greater and were numbered in millions instead of thousands—and the armies were all set on destruction. Destruction was not limited to a narrow battlefield, because the war took place in Russia, the Balkans, Italy, Belgium and France. What was more, a new threat against civilization presented itself. Destruction could reach any spot because of the aeroplane. Its role in the war was not very great, but its potentialities were evident.

The subsequent fruits of the war were also depressing. The war brought about collapse. In the light of this collapse, it was most difficult to believe that nature was irrepressibly moving to an ever better world. The optimism of the prewar naturalism looked absolutely ridiculous. It was equally evident that nationalism was a dangerous vision of life. In consequence, Wilson's dream of internationalism was accepted and the League of Nations was born. However, Wilson had no dynamism available to make the League work other than parliamentarism, a device which was nationalistic by tradition and which could be used without giving right reason or the common good a place. The League did not destroy nationalism, because the only instrument to make it work was nationalism. The world suddenly saw that parliamentarism was not a dyke against injustice and unreason, and many men became disgusted with it.

The collapse of Europe did not mean the destruction of Europe; it merely demanded reconstruction. But construction needs a plan, and a plan supposes a vision. The old vision went down in the collapse and something new had to take its place. The molding of the new vision is the work of our moment, for with the collapse of the West in 1918, a new era was born, and that era is our moment. The collapse had shown clearly that the unshakeable values of the prewar era were not unshakeable at all. Some were shaken right out of existence, and those which still remained had an anemic look. If the war shook the world materially and spiritually, the postwar years shook the modes of society. Nothing was considered valuable just because it had been around for a long time. Every value was questioned, and every questioning brought forth some answer, and answers were respectable only if they went counter to what had been believed before.

Class distinction became odious, and tended to disappear mainly because excess wealth was being confiscated by society. Naturalism was subjected to criticism. The result was that some dropped it altogether and returned to the older religious views. Karl Barth taught an utter unworldliness, based on despair for the world and a blind trust in God, who leads and meets the individual in ineffable fashion. A French group composed of men like Paul Claudel, Jacques Maritain, Charles Péguy, Ernest Psichari, found a rescue for thought and vision in the Catholic metaphysics of the Middle Ages rather than in the agnostic positivism of the prewar years. Movements of this kind could be found everywhere, but they never became torrential. The Catholic Church, after the bankruptcy of her erstwhile foes, took on a new vigor and a new respectability as manifest in writers like Chesterton and Belloc. Yet her new respectability and renewed strength did not make her determinant anywhere.

The sincere naturalists themselves re-examined their positions, and found out that it was better to drop the dogma of inevitable progress, and they substituted in its stead the notion of free collaboration of man with science in order to bring about Utopia. They admitted that things did not get better of themselves; man had to make them better, and man could fail in the task. However, only through positivistic naturalism could man make them better. This message was not as consoling as the old one, but it still had its comfort, for at least it left us with the illusion that we could of ourselves, without aid from without, save mankind by the simple process of looking at reality without prejudices and then construct it in accord with our desires. Failures might come, but by failure we learned. Error was now very important. It should not be the cause of despair, but only a way of learning to make all things better. Trial and error by the scientific method, that was the new naturalism. It was a new optimism, subtle and vague. We no longer were told that heaven will come, come what may, but rather heaven can come if we only put our minds and wills to it.

Prewar naturalism had been too deeply entrenched in society for it to disappear. It stayed on as the prevailing mood, though it came forth in a different dress. Though it stayed, it was not as proud as before, and it knew that many were looking at it with suspicion and hostility.

When parliamentarian internationalism failed, nationalism also came back. The old nationalism was willing to be a copartner with scientistic naturalism, but the new one wished to be its lord, using it for ends which were not subject to any rational control at all. It first rose up in languid Italy, and made that people buzz. It then raised its head in Germany, galvanizing a nation from lassitude into fever. The new nationalism developed technology but it had no use for scientism. Visions were formed by blind upsurges, divorced from reason. These visions pushed men to action, and for action they took advantage of technology. Parliamentarism was swept off the board, and arbitrary dictatorship of a small clique took its place. Nature was not God; God was not God; the Nation was the absolute demanding God, who would tolerate no gods beside himself. Fanaticism took the place of intelligence; passion was more important than reflection.

This was most unpalatable doctrine for the lands where naturalism was not tied to the service of nationalism. What is more, it was quite evident that the new nationalism would only wind up in war before reconstruction had been achieved. There could be no other outcome. Scientistic naturalism with its roots in the individualism of the past could hardly be kindly to totalitarian nationalism. However, it admired its own heresy, communism, as the older Marxist socialism was now called. Russia was being rebuilt along

Marxist lines. A literal following of the gospel according to Karl Marx proved impossible, and Nicolai Lenin made adaptations which seemed most un-Marxian and Joseph Stalin retreated more and more from the orthodox doctrine. Yet in Russia they were proceeding according to the naturalistic formula—trial and error. Science alone was given the role of directing life and constructing a new society. From the naturalistic point of view this was good, and if there were facets of communist society which appalled the men of the West, these were overlooked generously. After all, we must not be dismayed by errors. The principal thing was the progress that was being made. The Russians were marching toward Utopia on the right road, the road of scientistic naturalism. The academic people, the new professors of the world's theology, were all for Russia. In fact, many were of the opinion that naturalism must lead to communism—and they were probably quite right.

One effect of the collapse of Europe was a restlessness of the colonial territories. Asia was in a ferment. China was awakening and Japan became a world power with nationalism as its philosophy. Latin America realized that its situation was revolutionary, but the discontent of the masses was diverted from the true foe, local exploitation, by whipping up nationalism.

Everywhere the old *mores* fell to pieces. The Turks abolished the veil for their women. The East put on western clothes. Sex taboos were attacked in Europe and America. The financial crisis of 1929–1930 made the proletariat aware of the fact that the commonwealth could be tapped to give them comforts which previously had been acquired only by work. It was a time of confusion, uneasiness and insecurity. Nothing was stable. It came to a head in a new war which the nationalistic communities waged in the belief that the other nations were not strong enough to meet the flood of their passion rendered formidable by technology. The nationalistic powers were mistaken. The other peoples did still believe in something that was left over from the past, the dignity and liberty of the individual. In another orgy of destruction the struggle was waged with the total suppression of nationalism as an organized threat. The new struggle left all the European powers but Russia sick unto death. The United States alone had strength enough to take over the cause of freedom but the United States was neither ready for the role nor very willing to assume it. The colonial lands took advantage of the European debility, and they demanded successfully economic and political independence. Asia was in revolution and finally the Islamic lands followed its example.

This is the situation that faces mankind now. The West has not abdicated its ecumenical throne, but the throne is being fought for by two contestants. Communism is one claimant, which would regiment mankind dictatorially to a Utopia built ruthlessly on scientistic humanism, where nonconformism must pay the price of death. Against this force there is the other vision which is torn from within by two conflicting ideas: a love of liberty in terms of the worth of the individual person, and a faith in a deterministic naturalism as the only means for saving man. This latter vision is called democracy. In both camps the hunger for power is moving some reckless men to dominion and the struggle is not merely a clash of ideologies, but also a struggle between selfishnesses. It is a mistake to think that all that is taking place today is only a battle between two visions of man. Stubborn, cynical individuals, intoxicated by the prospect of power, are as much to blame as the divergent philosophies. On the other hand, we must not think that the struggle in the West is merely between two power groups, indifferent to ideologies. No man and no group can exercise power without a following, and people follow a man only in so far as he is the incarnation of an idea that satisfies them. The power seekers, willy-nilly, must propose a vision and to some degree must believe in it and try to realize it in history.

The tacit postulate of the two western forces is that whoever wins the West wins the East as well. This postulate is not as necessarily valid as the West unreflectively presumes. The Far East is not interested in our world views. The Middle East is quite indifferent to our philosophies. They are in a revolutionary moment, and by inner tensions they are exploding. If they watch the West, it is not because of the ideas of the West, but because of the threat or aid of the occident. The Chinese people is not communistic in its world view, even though its government is committed to the communistic theory, and as long as communism is not a general Chinese faith, China is not ideologically Marxist, though politically it has joined hands with Russia. The reason for the political gesture is the revolutionary desire of the Chinese to free themselves from exploitation and interference, which they identify with western rather than Russian influence. The Japanese are not democratic in the occidental meaning of that obscure term, but because of the revolutionary moment in their history they must join the western democracies to realize their own development, and as soon as they can, they will free themselves from the encumbering linkage to the West.

There are two enigmatic elements which help to confuse the general picture. First we note the rumblings of Islam which stretches continuously from the African Atlantic right across to the Philippine Islands in the Far Pacific. The Moslems are technologically unequipped but by that very fact they are also immune to a technological attack. Atom bombs in the desert neither hurt them nor aid their foe. Their loose organization prevents them from being crushed while their smoldering ardor can constantly break out over a wide area. The second element is the future of Latin America. The Latin continent is rich in raw materials of all kinds. Today the total Latin population is greater than the population of the United States. The Latin Americans are not yet developed industrially but are making impressive beginnings. They are divided within their lands and within the total Latin setup. The Latin Americans certainly have not come to any maturity, but who can say that this maturity cannot come sooner than we think? The latent dangers in the Southern continent are the deep *anti-Yanqui* feeling that is part of their culture and the strong instinct for arbitrary power that manifests itself in our Iberian neighbors.

As is evident from this rapid analysis, our moment is an unstable one. We are trying to construct an ecumenical framework that will be stable, but only instability faces us at home and abroad. What makes us especially uneasy is the lack of any general belief in a vision which could produce a common framework. We are materially advanced but we are spiritually retarded. This is a dreadful state, for in a lifetime it is possible to lose our material organization. We are all so narrowly specialized in our work and so dependent on other specialists that we would be helpless to take care of our ordinary needs if only a few industries were to fail. An automobile is useless if there is no gasoline, and if there are no refineries, crude oil cannot be changed into gasoline. Our large urban centers depend on intricate systems of communication, and New York would be emptied in a month if the railroads and trucks found no safe roads into the city. New Yorkers on the countryside would be sorry figures indeed. They would know nothing of the soil or animal husbandry;

they could not make the necessary tools, for they do not even know what they are. They could not spin nor weave. The tractors would rust in garages, mute symbols of a civilization that was knowledgeable but so rigidly organized that the failure of one part would destroy the whole, with no possibility of restoring itself.

The inertia that is characteristic of all things is also characteristic of man. Customs, habits, organizational patterns come and they can linger on even after the death of the idea that produced them. The Colosseum in Rome is still standing but it has not been used as a circus in 1500 years. Men today still have buttons on their sleeves, though the sleeves have not been open in a hundred years. Stable patterns for shifting variables, because of inertia, retain their stability in spite of the variability of the elements combined. Minor integrated patterns serve a general pattern, but a general pattern corresponds to a general idea. It can incorporate existing subsidiary patterns, and it must do so, because a complete reconstruction of all things relevant to man is humanly impossible. Yet the over-all pattern changes the meaning of the subsidiary patterns, and the over-all pattern is the product of a single vision of total reality. The tragic meaning of our moment is that its working vision of total reality is not creative. Scientistic humanism is not creative in spite of the fact that it was formed to be creative, for its formers overlooked a fundamental truth in humanity. The human being will not exert himself to be human, because he knows that he is human already. Naturalistic humanism urges man to be human and by human it means being comfortably what observation shows man to be. We are told to exert ourselves creatively to be what we evidently are. That is a meaningless message. We create only that which is not, and we enjoy, or adjust to, that which is. To make man work at the difficult task of being a man, you must urge him to be more than a man. Man can be moved efficaciously to action, only if by work he will be a superman, and between a superman and a godly man there is not much practical difference. To say that man is himself divine is something no man believes, for he knows that the divine is a richer thing than humanity. Even to tell a man to sweat, in order to be free like the gods, is not enough. You must tell him what he is to be free *for.* If he is told that he will be free from the marks of humanity—disease, imperfection, ignorance, fatigue, sorrow—he knows that this is not true. Naturalistic humanism asks man to lift himself by his bootstraps, and every attempt to apply this counsel will only bring about frustration. Naturalistic humanism can work temporarily only in a society where institutions of another time with a different vision are still operative by inertia. Once their saving action slows down to a halt, naturalistic humanism will have no power at all. It has a specious value, only because we overlook its killing weakness by ignoring it in the ordinary things of life, and in terms of those ordinary things we live. Yet the more popular naturalistic humanism becomes as a societal vision, the faster the old inherited institutions will collapse, for they were erected by a totally different vision.

The future of our moment is mysterious. It is certain that we are not going back to the world of 1912. It is not certain that we are not going back to 512 or 612. The predominant vision of naturalism is not going to save us, whether it be the naturalism that is willing to discard human freedom, or naturalism that wishes hopefully to retain it. If the men of our moment finally accept universally the religion of naturalism, we are doomed as was every moment that took that religion. Naturalism *is* a religion and it has a simple theology. If the naturalist explanation of God is correct, then God is something made to the image and likeness of man, and in the

universe there is nothing higher than man, and man is the
law of the universe. Man is God, and that the old Prophets
called idolatry, and they ridiculed it as nonsense.

Our liberal theologians, who adapt Christianity to naturalism, cannot help us by teaching that God is a way of
speaking of the deeper desires of the human heart. If this
were true, God still would be human, and that is still idolatry
in spite of its obscuring fuzziness.

Let me sum up the meaning of our moment. It is a time
whose mission is to reconstruct society, for the world of 1914
is gone. Ever since 1918 we have been trying to rebuild it.
We have patently not succeeded. The reason for our failure
is multiplex. One of the elements is that there are power-
hungry men effectively seizing dominion and using it to
satisfy their lust for more and more power. The faith
preached by these men is not the explanation of their action,
for with any or no faith they would continue their course,
which is dictated by instinct and not by intelligence. The
second element is the awakening of the vast colonial masses
to the general and effective realization that foreign direction
of their destinies is not to their advantage. Hence all of Asia,
much of Africa, and to a lesser degree Latin America, are
refusing the direction of the West. This awakening is not
caused by any *Weltanschauung* these peoples have, but results from the unhappy material condition in which they
find themselves. It is for them a revolutionary moment,
which inevitably came to birth. The third element is the
lack of a creative faith in the world at large, and of the
dominant West in particular. This would not be so disastrous
if communal effort would be guided by a vision, even though
not a genuine faith, yet effectively creative. *De facto,* the
West works on the basis of naturalistic humanism. It has
two conflicting forms: democratic naturalism, which wishes

to salvage large chunks of personal freedom from communal power, and communist naturalism which wishes to suppress any personal freedom in order to erect quickly and logically a stable, productive, economic framework whose automatic fruits would be a happy human life. Both of these forms are agreed on naturalistic humanism which basically announces that man's secular happiness is the sole concern of society and it is to be achieved by man's rational effort with no direction from any norm not derived from man's experience of himself. Material man is the absolute, and all other absolutes are only ideal projections of this man.

This naturalism is not universally accepted as a living faith. The colonial lands are only superficially committed to it. Even in the West, there are vital groups that reject it, and larger groups which use it pragmatically though they do not subscribe to it in terms of an inner conviction. Yet all groups, colonial and western, to some degree are infected enough by it to make naturalistic humanism the working vision of our time. This gives the power seekers their instrument, for they win to themselves the energies of the public by presenting themselves as incarnations of naturalism, which by default has usurped the place of a true faith in contemporary society. Many of our modern philosophers are defending, spreading and deepening this philosophy of life. Because of their work, this kind of thinking creates the atmosphere of the centers which formulate the intellectual commitments of the community.

As long as this philosophy is in the ascendency, our moment is a failure in its mission to construct the social configurations for a good life. The naturalistic vision can be propitious to the advance of technology, and the atom bomb, television and radar are the best proof that it is. However, it cannot give to men the will and the capacity to construct

a soul-saving society. The understanding of the atom can be
used for destruction just as it can be used for construction.
Naturalism cannot teach me how to use it for construction
as long as it tells me that the end of life is the fulfillment of
the desires derived from my instincts. Beyond these instincts
naturalism sees nothing, nor does it believe that they can be
controlled. Naturalism has brought forth a new and admirable science with which it hopes to handle the instincts,
namely psychiatry. However, a naturalistic psychiatrist does
not teach control of the instincts but only the adjustment
of instinctive drive to actual environmental conditions. The
naturalistic psychiatrist is as helpless to tell me where I must
go as any other naturalist. Frankly, he believes not that I go
anywhere but that I am carried to point "X," which he pi-
ously hopes will be better than point "Y," but he has no rational basis for this hope.

In the light of these reflections one can only be pessimistic.
If the present trend moves along its own course, eventually
there will only be chaos and then jungle life. Will humanity
follow this road? Who can say? Must it follow this road?
Definitely not. It can change its course at any time. It will
change its course sometime, at least once breakdown has shattered everything. Man has a stubborn impulse to live and
to live with his fellows. This very instinct will lead him to a
world view more constructive than naturalism. However, in
such a hypothesis, the change of views would not be in our
moment but in another.

What would lead us to a better world and a better use of
the technology at our command? Only the universal submission of man to an absolute, commanding, personal God, transcendental and infinitely greater than man. This message
drives the naturalists to fury, for it is their sincere belief that
this kind of god was slain in the last century, and a return to

him means obscurantist retrogression. The moment is too grave to permit dialectical controversy with such willful men. When you change roads and find that the new road is leading you to a swamp and not to a protecting city, you go back on the road to the point where the other road led elsewhere. You do not keep on the new road just because in the past some one deliberately chose to change paths. Change is not necessarily for the better, and only the Pollyanna attitude of the nineteenth century romantically believed that all change led to a greater good.

Why is the belief in God, transcendental and commanding, necessary for man? Because in society man must control his instincts. This he will not do, unless he lives in the firm conviction that laws have been made for him personally by a being with whom he cannot dispute, to whom he must joyfully submit. A police-state is no such being, for we know that the police-state is a human thing, and why should one man submit to another? He can be coerced, it is true, but universal coercion is the dehumanization of man and the ruin of society. The romantic naturalists think that they can achieve submission by enlightening men to the necessity of self-control, or as they put it, "adjustment," in order for men to live together, as men sincerely want to and always will. This is a pretty dream. Man will not control himself in terms of enlightened selfishness. Selfishness rejects control, and the more enlightened it is, the more ways it will find to escape control. Some romantic souls can achieve a high morality because morality is for them the supreme good, but humanity at large has no such love and respects morality grudgingly and not from loving spontaneity. Unless the average man recognizes that control is imposed on him by the Lord with whom he cannot debate and whose infinite power will avenge the violation of his will, man will not control himself. The community which wholeheartedly and integrally believes in a commanding transcendental God, needs no police force.

Belief in God is not sufficient, though it is fundamental. There is needed too a belief in a kind, wise and directing God. There is need of belief in a final human destiny greater than the momentary satisfaction of instincts. Such a belief will accept the inevitable shortcomings of life as part of a mission to work out a happier salvation. Wealth is not the goal which is important, neither is power, nor health, nor fame, nor pleasure. The important thing is to do the will of God who has planned things for our ultimate good and for the good of the whole. The prayer of such a believer is: Thy will be done. The practical plan of such a man is to seek first the Kingdom of Heaven and its righteousness, and he knows that then all things will work out well. Such a faith makes for the good life, the good society. Arts can thrive and science flourish. Calamities may come but they will not crush us. The resilience of the believer in God and in his righteousness permits him to move forward gladly, with joyful effort and inner tranquillity.

The sad thing is that though this faith, if shared by all the members of society, would make society a pleasant place indeed, yet it can never be accepted merely as a means of saving society. You cannot use the great religion as a means to something less than God. It is not a human means. It is a human end. All things subordinate to it; it does not subordinate to anything. A good society is its by-product and not its proper fruit. Consequently, even though my diagnosis of the moment be right, we cannot draw the conclusion: therefore let us preach a religious return to the transcendental Lord, architect, lawmaker and judge. No man will accept religion just to save society. Marx was so wrong in so many things. He taught that society made its religion. Just the opposite is true; religion makes its society. Men submit to God not because this is useful, but because they believe in the reality of God and recognize that it is logical to submit to him, and illogical to refuse submission. This faith takes place in society but it is not a socially produced experience. It is the meeting of God and man, a fearful but wholesome experience. Society does not lead men to it, though it unwittingly offers many an occasion.

Therefore my suggestion for the saving of our moment is not a practical one. You cannot whoop up a campaign in favor of religion in order to save the world. No one will accept religion for that motive. You can only give testimony to the truth of the universal permeation of reality with a transcendental God to whom man must submit, gladly and totally, because this is true and not for any other reason. If such testimony were to be generally received, society would save itself, but there is no way of making man receive it. The way to save our society is to go beyond society in search of the Kingdom of God and its righteousness, and then all the other things will be added unto us. If society will not do this, at least the individual can.

3

✛✛✛

The Role of Religion
in American Society

✛✛✛

THE HEBREW prophet (Jeremiah 8:11) said: "They have healed the wound of my people lightly, saying, 'Peace, peace' when there is no peace." These enigmatic words sound relevant to every age. Men always and everywhere desire peace, but they find it either absent or insecure.

The philosophers and psychologists have been rather pessimistic as to the degree of peace possible for man. They suggest that absolute peace is a mere dream, incapable of total actualization. Some go so far as to think that total peace would be harmful for man who functions best in the presence of challenge and under the stimulus of the demands of the battle for survival.

The historians tend to confirm the pessimism of the philosophers and psychologists. They show that peace is very relative in the chronicles of our kind. There are periods of blazing war causing destruction and widespread suffering. Other periods can be called times of cold war, which are simultaneously periods of cold peace. I am told by Filipinos

42

that the Japanese during the occupation of the Philippine Islands divided all non-Japanese into three classes: the Americans and English were hostile enemies; the Spaniards were neutral enemies; the Germans and Italians were allied enemies. In short, all who were not Japanese were simply enemies. Such a mentality sees in every alien a foe and feels that the nation is in constant universal war. With such an attitude, there is no peace, no matter how much men may shout the word.

There is another situation described by historians. It was the time of the *pax Romana,* the Roman peace of the Caesars. Yet so discerning a mind as Tacitus could criticize it by making a non-Roman say: *solitudinem faciunt et pacem appellant* (they make a desert and then call it peace).

Now what is peace? Perhaps no one answered that question better than St. Augustine who defined it as the serene stability of order. The regular wheeling of the planets about their axes and about the sun is peace. The regular rise of the flowers in the spring and their death in the fall is peace. We can count on these things. We can adjust to them with security. We can depend on them. They will not get in our way and we can plan our own activity relying on their support.

Nature is regular because it is a manifestation of necessity. Hence our problem comes principally from man. He is free, and he can abuse his freedom as well as use it. We cannot tell what any individual man will do in an individual context. We have moral codes which should regulate man's behavior but there is no infallible way of making man live up to our laws. The result is that our peace is always threatened. Moral principles are abstract; concretely their actualization works out as a brittle arrangement rather than a stable order.

Our task is to change that brittle arrangement into a serene stability. Then we truly shall have peace. We are realistic enough to expect something less than utopian perfection, but we still want enough of stability in the patterns of a man's action so that we can count on it, so that we can freely act among our neighbors with confidence and trust.

The adolescent mind whether on young or old shoulders sees an easy way to achieve this stability. With an adequate police force applying coercive pressures on people, the brittle codes will become firm. In a word, shoot all the miscreants. This is a police-state's answer to the problem. Yet history teaches that it does not work. To implement such policy, you need a mighty police force which means a great expense to the community. Then, too, who will police the police? Even if it works for a short period, we have transformed our earthly habitat into a jail. In jails there is a feasible facsimile of a serene stable order, but the price is the loss of liberty. But we want order to give us liberty and not to end it. This must be stressed. We desiderate an order which guarantees liberty but not all orders favor freedom. An order which is spontaneously accepted by the community is no threat to independent action but the order which is maintained by violent coercion enslaves man. Slavery, in the strict sense of the word, is inhuman because man is born to be free.

The real problem which faces us, then, is how to induce a spontaneous order obtaining all over the world. Now it is useless to expect governments to produce it. Governments work by law and its execution through police power. The State, therefore, looks to the exterior behavior of man, for the police cannot get at his invisible mind. The State can try to persuade but it is not equipped to achieve persuasion without fail. Schools and the social media of suggestion can be monopolized by governments, but they cannot control the spirit of man without his consent. The police can throw our bodies into jails; they can torture us into specious submission —but they cannot hold on to the soul which flows through the torturer's grasping fist. It is the indestructible free spirit of man which ultimately unseats the tyrant, for the tyrant cannot crush it because he cannot touch it. That is why no tyranny can look forward to an indefinite survival. Man is weak but there is an inherent toughness in his soul which defies material onslaughts, and, in the long run, the tyranny will tire of its exhausting effort to force the soul to be what it will not be.

The State therefore cannot cause a spontaneous stable order, for its own dynamism will function effectively only if the order is already there. But the State is not the only form of community in human life. Before the states were, the religions are, and these appear as fellowships. The religious community, unlike the State, looks to the inner life of men. If it deals with the external, it does so only because the external is the visible overflow of inward vision and will. The strength of religion is not derived from any police power. All religions have this in common that they move the inward will through the excitation of an inward vision. The sharper the vision, the more dynamic is the influence of the religion on the will and behavior of the believer.

Society, in consequence, has the means to produce the spontaneous serene order it needs for its own survival and well-being. These means are the churches. In America, then, secular society must look to its religious communities for its civic welfare. The secular affairs of men will not move fruitfully unless the secular order leans on the spiritual.

Here we are faced with a startling paradox. Secular and spiritual are terms of opposition. Secular by its concept is set up against the spiritually eternal. And yet the secular will not flourish without acceptance of the spiritual.

Paradoxes cause difficulties. Man's urge to simplification

looks for centric unity and paradox is the assertion of polarity. It has therefore always been a tendency in men to try to reduce polarity to monism, because monism is easier for the finite mind to grasp. It takes healthy mental balance to steer smoothly in a paradoxical situation.

The attempts to reduce the secular-spiritual paradox to monism have obviously been in two directions. The older reduction was the incorporation of the secular into the religious, so that the State was a function of the Church. The autonomous secular community disappeared and the Church managed the secular affairs of its religious fellowship. In certain circumstances, this is a viable solution—but those circumstances are so rare that normally the absorption of the secular interests into the domain of religious brotherhood causes social malaise. It was not without reason that such great religious thinkers as St. Augustine and Thomas Aquinas insisted that the religious community could not eliminate the secular community by reason of the very needs of man. Both communities must be there. One alone will leave mankind crippled.

The reduction of the State to the status of a department in a religious society is not our danger today. In almost every nation religion is pluralistic. This very fact poses a grave problem to the men of state, for one of the elements which formerly consolidated the secular society was its religious homogeneity. Today religion is a divisive force in our commonwealths. In consequence it is literally impossible to make secular society a mere epiphenomenon of a religious fellowship, because every religion is a minority in the national community nor is any one the whole.

The danger in our time is the relegation of religion to the status of a function of the secular order. We have passed out of the period when there was a serious effort to extirpate re-

ligion from the lives of men. From 1800 to 1940 it was the
naïve belief of many thinkers that religion was a relic of past
ignorance and weakness. Through the knowledge marvel-
lously accumulated by modernity's fruitful sciences man's
needs were being adequately met. Religion had nothing to
contribute to sated man. Secular organization, thanks to
science, could solve all human problems. Such a position
was possible in the good old days of the war between science
and religion. Communism, the colossal destructiveness of
atomic energy released for us by science itself, the failures of
all essays to produce a moral code on the basis of scientific
empiricism made the war between religion and science as
irrelevant to our time as the phrenology which was born
in the same age. Today scientist and man of religion both
see clearly that we need both science and faith, and the few
who have failed to make the recognition strike us as pathetic
survivals of a simpler past.

What is happening today is well stated by Will Herberg
(*Protestant—Catholic—Jew*. New York: Doubleday, 1955).
According to this brilliant and sensitive observer, American
secularism, far from rejecting or ignoring religion, has taken
it to its bosom. Americans in general think religion is a good
thing, and the main reason seems to be that it helps citizens
to be better citizens. A religious man is prone to be an honest
man, a man who will keep his word and do his duty. He will
be sober, industrious and patriotic. These are qualities which
the nation needs, and since religion produces them, this
nation is for religion.

Here then we have a frank recognition of the truths we
saw earlier. The secular order needs peace which means a
serene stable order. Such order can only be produced by the
free inner consent of men to abide by the order. The wider
and deeper the conviction, the smaller is the need of a numerous and expensive police force. Religion makes for un-

selfishness and disciplined freedom. What militia and con-
stables cannot achieve, is the inevitable achievement of a
genuinely felt faith.

It seems, then, that the role of religion in America is to
produce the virtues which the secular community needs and
which it cannot produce itself. Certainly the modern secularist sees it this way.

Yet is this the answer to the question of the role of the
American Churches? Are the American Churches here to
save America?

Before we answer these questions, we must make some
preliminary observations. Take the simple sentence: He came
to complete a foursome for a game of bridge. That sentence
is ambiguous. It may mean that he came with the purpose
that there be four people in order to facilitate the playing of
bridge. It may also mean that he came and as a result there
were four people present and a bridge game could be started.
Now there is a world of difference between these two meanings. In both cases we have a bridge game. But in one case
the completion of the foursome was a by-product of the
advent of the man who had quite a different purpose in coming. In the other case the completion of the quartet was the
intention which moved the man to arrive.

We must distinguish between purpose and consequent,
between function and by-product. If the modern campaign
to interest our people to take up religion seriously is orien-
tated to the secular good of our community, a disservice is
rendered to religion and the effort itself is futile. Of course
it is true that if the overwhelming majority of Americans become devout members of the churches in our land, a high
degree of civic virtue will result. It is even true that if they
do not engage in religion in some form or other we have
reason to become pessimistic about our national safety. De-

votion to the community supposes a spirit of sacrifice and high self-discipline. Such qualities are produced, at least for the majority of mankind, by religion alone. There are a distinguished few who can be virtuous because of abstract natural ideals or esthetic appeals, but such men and women are not numerous enough to be the guarantee of the nation's survival. History has shown that it is religion which inculcates virtue in the mass of men, and there is no substitute for it.

But the fact is that if you seek your soul you will lose it. If you lose it, you will find it. Religion, in any form it takes, is a recognition of the lordship of an absolute to whom or which man must bow. This submission, free and inward, is the root of the virtues of unselfishness and self-restraint. Few are the men who can practice virtue because it is its own reward. All who effectively accept God will be committed at least in principle to a life of virtue because God wills it. Thy will be done is one of the key orientations of the Lord's Prayer.

The individual needs the community in order to be an individual but, in spite of that, there will necessarily be a conflict between individual and collectivity. The individual often desires passionately things which are not for the common weal. The individual in these circumstances will not restrain his passion just because it is good for the community. There must be a power and a glory above self and the collectivity to move the individual efficiently to curb himself. Nor will the individual accept such an absolute only because it is good for the whole. The love of neighbor stems from some kind of love of God. But you cannot kneel down before God just because society requests or demands it. You may kneel but it will not be before God. The submission to God, the very heart of religion, is not pressured from the outside. It is the answer to a call heard in the inmost secrets of the soul. What is more, the man who becomes religious for secular gain is not genuinely religious but most irreligious. The religious assent is the unconditional surrender to the Ground of Being. It is not a calculated investment for temporal dividends. God's ways are not man's ways, and the goods he gives us in love may not be the seeming goods we desire.

Hence the role of the churches in America is not to save America. The day they make that their purpose, they have failed as churches. The role of the churches is to be the locus where man meets God and dedicates himself to do His purposes. When I see a flag in a church, though not against it, I often wonder if its presence is not the sign that we are more anxious about the fatherland than the Father's will.

As a conclusion of this meditation I would suggest that we be wary of the current pressure on us to be religious. It is urging us to a good thing for a bad reason. Religion is good just because it is religion. It is not good because it is good for my country. It would be good even if my country drew from it no benefit whatever. It may indeed be true that the good of the country requires a more widespread religious response of our people, but that can neither make our people religious nor be a valid motive for church affiliation.

Recognizing this basic truth, it still remains to be said that given a stronger religious dedication by our national society, our secular affairs will move better. In fact, I would go so far as to say that things will go badly if we do not first seek the Kingdom of God and His righteousness. Given that seeking, all other things will be added on to us. But what we seek must be the Kingdom of God and not the other things.

4

✤✤✤

Catholic Communication
with the World

✤✤✤

ONE OF the massive facts in the actual world is the existence
of a society called the Roman Catholic Church. I must insist
that the massive fact is that Roman Catholicism is a society.
Of course, it is also a religion; it is a world view; it is a factor
in culture, politics and every phase of interhuman relations.
But the basic human truth about the Catholic Church is
that it is an autonomous society. It is because of this reason
that the Catholic Church is so different from older religions
like Judaism, which is no society though it embraces distinct
societies. Hence it is also different from communism which
is a world view but not a society, even though the Union of
the Russian Soviet Socialist Republics is a society and to
this degree is like the Catholic Church, but the communists
in the non-Russian lands rarely belong to that society no
matter how much they may admire it.

Now one of the basic difficulties confronting a social group
is to make itself understood to those who are not of it. This
difficulty need not be vexing to a loose collectivity if the

members are unconcerned about an alien conception of their reality. Many a mathematician doesn't give a fig because nonmathematicians cannot understand his craft. Understood or misunderstood, most mathematicians go their merry way quite content. Such an attitude is impossible for the Catholic. While the mathematician is not obliged in logic to make all men mathematicians, the Catholic actually must desire that every human being become a Catholic.

Any society is to some degree closed so that the world can be validly divided by the logical opposition of the members and nonmembers of the given society. Unless a nonmember clearly sees advantages in entering into the narrower circle of the given organization, he will not seek admission. His field of possibilities is larger outside of the community than in it. A society dynamized by a strong proselytizing nisus is therefore necessarily anxious to show nonmembers the advantages of belonging to its fellowship. Logically, in consequence, a problem of communication is created.

Many a naïve Catholic is amazed and puzzled by the fact that the majority of the world does not wish to enter into the Catholic Church. As the Catholic sees it, the Church is the supreme elevation of man into the participation of the divine nature. Hence, it seems to him unintelligible that any man should not want this great good. Yet the patent fact for everyone is that most men show either indifference, annoyance with, or even hostility to the Catholic Church. With this fact facing the Catholic, he is not only logically but existentially forced to consider the problem of communication. It is obvious that the greater part of the world does not see in Catholicism what the Catholic sees. He must therefore explain the Church in his encounter with men.

The rise of semantics in our time is the fruit of the recognition of the complexities involved in human communication. The older generations quite blithely counseled us to say what we meant, and then we would be understood. The tacit assumption was that a good dictionary and an adequate grammar would enable us to communicate. However, the studies of the Freudian psychologists, the logical positivists, the existentialists have shown us that so simplistic a belief is altogether inadequate as a starting point in the solution of the problem of communication.

For the Catholic there is an added urgency for effective communication. We are living in a pluralistic world. Our secular society, wherever it is found, is made up of members with different world views. Except in some isolated pockets, there is no homogeneity of beliefs anywhere in the world. Yet we must all live together, and we are all anxious to live in such a way that there will be peace and harmonious collaboration in our coexistence. Hence communication cannot be exclusively directed to conversion. It must more often be an apologetic task so that the great society we live in will be able to deal with us wisely and gently. Catholic communication is a task not only because it is demanded by the smaller Catholic society to which the Catholic belongs but also because it is required by the larger secular society in which he is inexorably situated. This recognition is frankly made today by Catholics. Many non-Catholics are not aware that the Catholics have made it, and they think that the Catholic is still committed to the older vision that secular society and religious society are materially identical as they were in the Western Europe of the Middle Ages.

Any particular group erects a language and a set of symbols of its own. This enterprise is usually unrecognized by the group itself because it is superficially using the same semantic instrument as the larger community in which it exists. Yet the jargon of the schoolboy is not the same language spoken by the general community. Words are used differently and the language is restricted to a small part of its possibilities. Even within a family, certain words are symbols, in a sense, not recognizable by those beyond the family circle.

This inevitable situation affects Catholicism in a special way. Perhaps the most eloquent instance is the English Bible tradition. Many believe that the Reformation broke up the medieval unity of Western Europe. Certainly Hilaire Belloc seemed to think so. However, the truth of the matter seems to be that the Reformation merely manifested an already existing division of Europe, a division it did not produce but which produced it. The Reform is as much an effect of parochial nationalism as of religious preoccupations. When Luther and Tyndale translated the Bible they were championing the rights of the local dialects of Christendom against the ecumenical Latin which was less vital than the local tongues. The Catholic translators of Douay and Rheims bring this out unconsciously. Whereas Tyndale and Coverdale Englished the Scriptures thoroughly, the Douay translators did it in such a way that much of the ancient Latin survived. In many expressions they merely transliterated the Latin, ignoring the English word which carried the same idea. The Douay interpreters were speaking simultaneously *urbi et orbi,* to their Catholic peers and to all English-speakers at large. This double objective for the same effort necessarily produced ambiguity. But the ambiguity was not contradiction. The Catholic had to speak the Catholic language which was his for a thousand years. The non-Catholics, on the other hand, were free to use the new language of their moment.

This predicament confronts the Catholic today no less than in the days of the sixteenth century. The non-Catholics are always very much of their time, much more so than the Catholics. Non-Catholic theologians use existentialist ter-

minology in our era, though only fifty years ago such a terminology was universally unknown. The Catholics do so likewise but clumsily and with reluctance. The new language is
not natural to them, and they speak it with an alien accent.
Much of existentialist terminology was actually borrowed
from Scholasticism, and when the Catholic uses the word
"existence," it does not make him think of phenomenology
but rather of medieval metaphysics. The Catholic cannot
help himself, for he is a conditioned being like all others. It
will be the convert to Catholicism who will use the new
language with ease and grace but he will be understood
better by non-Catholics than by his fellow Catholics. This
is clearly the situation in the case of Gabriel Marcel.

There are three areas of human existence which embar-
rass Catholics in their efforts at communication. This embar-
rassment may be interpreted by many as a sign of inadequacy
in the Catholic answer to questions of deep concern. However, this need not be the case. In any given moment the
tendency of men is to ignore one pole of a bipolar problem.
When this happens, one particular answer seems simpler and
obvious. Those who keep both poles in view cannot give
this easy answer but their appeal to bipolarity is not successful because in the given moment, people at large myopi-
cally overlook one of the poles. With time, the existence of
the second pole will be recognized but by that time the question no longer arouses any felt urgency.

The first area where communication is difficult is the field
of modernity. Every generation esteems its own insights
highly and feels only for its own formulation of its problems.
What is modern is not only modern but by easy assumption
can be assumed to be the wave of the future. By a kind of
Oedipus complex the past is hated. Yet the present is much
more the past than it is the future. But there is a thrill in

being modern, for individual existence can be nothing else than modern; it is only now. It is society rather than the individual which has the consciousness of the past. Its very modern existence is also an affirmation of history. Hence, the Catholic Church looks simultaneously to the past and to the present. It is never a commitment simply to the present. This causes much malaise because in any given moment the past is suspect.

Yet at any time there is a paradoxical quality in the devotion to modernity. The past despised is the immediate past rather than the period of remote origins. Modernity can make peace with the archaic but not with the last generation. In fact, the archaic can take on a glow and a glory inspiring awe in moderns. The Golden Age is deep in the past which the immediate future must recapture. It was the blind willful men of the last few generations who were the spoilers. In this situation the Catholic Church is again at a disadvantage. Not only does she affirm the past but, with equal vigor, she affirms the community of the past with the present. She will not iconoclastically destroy what is at hand in favor either of the remote past or of the presumed future.

Modernity is atomistic. Catholicism is a continuum. Hence, the Church is always antimodern. This makes communication difficult in the modern moment, which, of course, is any actual moment. Modern is a word that a wise speaker will try to avoid. So many things of history were labeled in the past as modern. Yet it is ludicrous today to refer to them by the label they chose. The theological modernism of the turn of the century is hardly modern now and the *theologia moderna* of the late fifteenth century was so little modern a century later that the use of the word is sheerly nominal.

There is loss and gain in every finite event. The antimodernism of the Church gives her an advantage in history. During the last two decades of the nineteenth century and the first two decades of the twentieth, the *Syllabus of Errors* of Pio Nono was a scandal to the world. It was so antimodern. The Pope was flying into the face of the future. Non-Catholics were angered by the Syllabus and even Catholics were embarrassed. Yet, when we read the document today, we wonder what all the uproar was about. It sounds now as a pronouncement, by and large, quite acceptable to contemporary men. The reason for this change is that the optimistic and rationalistic liberalism of the nineteenth century is no longer modern. It is "old hat," a delirium of the perverse last generation. We are reminded of Will Herberg's use of Hansen's principle: What the son wishes to forget, the grandson wants to remember. The stubborn opposition of the Church to communism was embarrassing in the 'twenties and 'thirties, when it was quite the thing to be at least a fellow traveler. Today, no apology need be made for that opposition. In fact, today, the polemicist must accuse the Church of being as bad as communism, just as twenty years ago he insisted she was not as good.

However, the advantage of the Church's antimodernism is slight in comparison with its disadvantage for communication. It is a hard and awkward task to be ever forced to be uncommitted to the passing superstitions and frenzies of the moment we live in. Contemporaries see in such an aloofness a refusal to belong—and that is always an exasperating thing for the one who enthusiastically belongs. Nor is it an easy thing to hold dialogue with an exasperated man.

This difficulty is intensified by the presence of a traditional vocabulary of long standing. The Catholic language was formed gradually over the centuries, keeping the points of view of past moments of history. The completely modern man does not know this symbolic system, nor does he feel any desire to learn it. When he does hear it spoken, he is prone to misunderstand it. In consequence, the Catholic is always bilingual; he must speak his own traditional tongue, for only by it can he live his own traditional life, and he must also translate this language to the men of his day. Bilingualism is always an obstacle because no one actually speaks two languages with the same ease and fluency. One of the two languages is the individual's proper vehicle of communication while the other is a submission to a social necessity, resented rather than loved.

The antimodernism of the Catholic Church, therefore, always hampers the Catholic in his essays of communication. The second obstacle need not be so perennial, though it functions powerfully in our time. The Catholic, *qua* Catholic, is socially specified because the Church is a society. To be social puts man under authority, for anarchism simply liquidates all social bonds. Now authority is restrictive, even when the restrictions themselves are life-giving. And there are revolutionary moments in history when authority is resented and freedom extolled. We are in such a moment and the word "authoritarian" is for us a bad word.

"Authority" is a most ambiguous term. It means so many things. Perhaps the common denominator of all its uses is the notion of power. "By what authority" means, "by what power." Not all authority is arbitrary, for there is an intellectual authority with no element of voluntarism in it. When we say that in a certain field a man speaks with authority, we are saying that he knows his field. He thus becomes an authority. A witness likewise speaks with authority though his witness function is purely informative. He is a man who knows because he experienced what he relates. He gives no other proof for his testimony than the fact that he experienced what he says.

Any religious statement rests on some authority. It cannot

rest on a referral to measurable public data of the empirical order because God is not of that order. Christianity has from the beginning recognized this truth. The Christian evangelists gave witness to God's good news in Jesus. Witness was the only thing they could give. The dialectic of the Greek philosophers offered no means for the authorization of their message.

Christianity today is far removed in time from the witness of the associates of Jesus. The authority of their witness can only be mediated to us. There are current three generic theories concerning this mediation. The Christians of the Reform tradition look on the Bible as their decisive mediator. The Oriental Orthodox find the medium in the spontaneously surviving and evolving traditions of a community. The Catholics believe that their society, as a living and structured organism, mediates the testimony. In Catholicism it is not a book which has the ultimate authority nor yet the floating traditions of a loosely conjoined fellowship. It is the living community itself, acting as a society with the proper hierarchical architectonic of a mystical body. Yet none of the three forms of Christianity pretends to speak without authority.

What prejudices contemporary man against the Catholic form of authority is that it is juridical. If an organized society itself is to be the decisive mediation of the Gospel, it must be jurisdictionally operative. Yet the consequence will be that belief seems to be imposed by fiat and bureaucracy. Both in the Reform churches and Eastern Orthodoxy there is fullest possibility for a personal reconstruction of the Gospel. In Catholicism this possibility is severely restricted. This restriction seems to many to be an assault on freedom. Consequently, the witness of the Church grates on the sensitivities of our time.

The non-Catholic Christian has two questions: what does

the Church say, and what does God say? These questions are
for him two, and the answer to the one is not necessarily the
answer to the other. For the Catholic, the two questions are
identical in scope, because he believes that God speaks exclusively through the Church, so that what God says and
what the Church says in his name are necessarily one. He
believes this because he believes that only the Church can
tell us what God communicates to the world and time. But
in dialogue with non-Catholic Christians this basic assumption cannot be shared by the non-Catholic. When the Catholic proves that this or that proposition is taught by the
Church, the Catholic has done all he considers required. But
when the non-Catholic, spontaneously and with no malice,
immediately asks what God says on the same subject, the
Catholic is inwardly amazed by what he deems to be an irrelevant question. He antecedently rejects the notion that
one could know God's word except by the teaching of the
Church. The two participants in the dialogue are at cross-
purposes without even being aware of it. This explains the
futility of the old-fashioned polemic between Catholic and
non-Catholic, with the Bible acting as a court of appeals.
The non-Catholic understood the Bible through his sincere,
sometimes scholarly, but always personal reconstruction of
what the Bible says. The Catholic understood the Bible as
his living fellowship interpreted it. Such debate was no debate because there was no common ground to make a dialogue viable. The Bible in its material reality seemed to
keep the two disputants together but the material Bible is
just one more isolated fact in the universe, incapable of
uniting anything. It is the formal Bible, the Bible understood, which can be the link of union between two men.
When the understandings are different, there is no union.
There is not even one Bible, but two. This is clear in the

Protestant controversy between fundamentalists and non-fundamentalists.

The inevitable authoritarianism of Catholicism makes communication with antiauthoritarians difficult for the Catholic. The Catholic must always begin his dialogue with an exposition of the meaning of the Church. Nor will he consider this a question permitting any answer except the affirmation of the Catholic Church. That is his Christian faith. There he stands; he cannot do otherwise. The non-Catholic Christian, by the very fact of being non-Catholic, coldly or warmly bridles at the Catholic conception of Christianity, even when he understands it. When he doesn't understand it, he is simply mystified by the Catholic's position. The Protestant begins his conversation unconsciously supposing that the Catholic comes to Christianity in the Protestant way. He cannot help himself in this approach to the question, but the approach makes fruitful dialogue most problematical. It will take much reflection for the Protestant to realize that he is as authoritarian as the Catholic but in a different way. Although, like the Catholic, he follows an authority and a tradition, he will accuse the Catholic of authoritarianism and traditionalism without realizing that he too bases his beliefs on these two grounds.

The ecumenical movement in our day is a great effort to facilitate communication. However, it is a Protestant movement. The postulates of the meetings are tacitly Protestant. The free examination of the historical sources of the Christian religion is the *modus operandi*. But the question to be faced is not a historical but a religious one. Christianity is a historical phenomenon but its problems are not to be solved historiographically. Religious assent derives from the God-encounter of the individual man, conditioned by grace, his growth and environment. Two sincere men interpret his-

torical evidence differently because all interpretation begins
with principles outside the field of evidence. These initial
principles are the real dynamism of inference.

The third obstacle to effective Catholic communication is
the Catholic's social conception of the Gospel. He believes
that the commitment to God implies a commitment to the
people of God. He does not think that God can be adequately known or properly served except in the holy community, which is indestructibly holy because it is God's way
to salvation, not because its members are all necessarily holy.
Man's salvation is man's ultimate quest and imperative. All
else is secondary and subsidiary to this primatial concern.
The result is that there is a possible conflict between the
authority of the secular community to which the Catholic belongs and the authority of the divine community of which he
is also a member. This produces the famous problem of the
relations between Church and State.

The non-Catholic who knows something about Catholic
ecclesiology discovers that his Catholic neighbor confronts
the secular problems of the political collectivity with Catholic persuasions. This frightens him. He rarely reflects that
he approaches the same problems with a Protestant or Orthodox or Jewish persuasion. This frightens the Catholic. With
these two frights to confuse the issue, communication becomes ambiguous. The Witness of Jehovah refuses to bear
arms in a purely secular war. The Quaker refuses to bear
arms for any cause. The Methodist and the Baptist try to
outlaw alcoholic drinks in the secular community. The
Southern public school teaches a Protestant version of Christianity, at least by implication. Yet somehow these things do
not produce great malaise in the American body politic. But
the Catholic's idiosyncracies are always more alarming.

The naturalist has a solution for all this. He demands that

the individual citizen accept the authority of the political commonwealth as ultimate and final. The democratic naturalist supposes that this authority operates through a process of the showing of hands, so that the will of 51 per cent of the community is the law even for the 49. He allows every member of the collectivity to think and act as he pleases until the authority of the majority has become legally declared. Then the individual must bow not to God but to Columbia, the gem of the ocean.

As many religious non-Catholics have seen, the naturalist solution of the conflicts between the secular community and religion is not acceptable to any religious person. They have recognized that we cannot be ready to render to Caesar the things which are God's. Whenever the demand has been made, men of faith—Catholic, Protestant, Jew, Muslim, Buddhist—have refused to obey, even if their disobedience spelled death. These deaths have always been regarded by men at large as noble things, but the naturalistic statist, at least in theory, must consider them evil.

In spite of the incompatibility of the naturalist view with religious conviction, there is a tendency in this country even among religious people to accept the naturalist theory. The reason is obvious enough. The majority of the land is Protestant, even though many millions are not church-affiliated. They know in consequence that the 51 per cent of the nation will not demand something contrary to their own none-too-clear religious tenets. The only ones threatened are the Catholics, Jews and Orthodox. The rising power of any one of these groups alarms the general Protestant majority. If they are to lose their majority status, they will not enjoy the security they now have. Fear and resentment will be their attitude to the growing minority.

How can the Catholic adequately explain his position to such a majority? It is a formidable task. The Catholic talks theory and ideal democracy but the non-Catholic concentrates on practical consequences, often enough not logically entailed by the theory expounded. The Catholic must insist that he does not put the body politic above his religious community. The non-Catholic believer really makes the same profession but since he is in the majority, he does not have to insist on it. The Catholics at present are involved in the task of making their position intelligible to the total secular community. Some of the Catholics do not want any change of rhetoric in their basic doctrines, while others do want such a change. The position of the latter is most uncomfortable. They are suspected in their own fellowship; nor are they properly understood by the men beyond it. There comes for them a temptation, understandable enough, to drop the whole thing.

In the light of the observations so far made, it would seem that communication for the Catholic to those outside his communion is highly precarious. There are Catholics who think that this is more than a seeming and rather the objective reality. They make no attempt to communicate effectively. However, there are facets of the phenomenon which make us slow to accept such a simplistic and pessimistic position.

The Catholic in the pluralistic world of today is more than a witness to the Gospel. He is also a neighbor to those who do not accept his witness. As a neighbor, he has the Christian duty to love his fellow even though he be a Samaritan. The coexistence of Catholic and non-Catholic cannot tolerate high walls around their several estates. The coexistence involves human fusion and this fusion is impossible if some degree of mutual understanding is not achieved. The Catholic wants to and has to belong to his pluralistic milieu. He has no designs against it. He wishes that all were of his

Church but he is realistic enough to know that they are not nor will they be so in any foreseeable future. Actually many of the Catholic's beliefs are shared by those not of the household of his faith. The Catholic loves his secular community and makes the same sacrifices for it as his non-Catholic compatriot, even though his position in it is not as secure. There is also a thing called reason and all men are reasonable in some measure, no matter what their religion be, even though nobody, Catholic or non-Catholic, is altogether reasonable. Given the force of prejudice in all things human, a stronger union is spontaneously possible between Catholic and Protestant than between either and a Jew. Again, Jew and Christian can certainly unite more easily than either with a Buddhist. These are basic facts whether we like them or not. The general friendliness of Jews and Catholics in this country, in contrast to their hostilities in other lands, is explained by the fact that here they both are minorities defending themselves against a majority bigger than both of them combined.

The problem of communication across the Catholic-non-Catholic barrier falls primarily on the Catholic. In a lesser way it puts some obligations on the non-Catholic.

The Catholic has no right to expect the majority of his secular community to speak and understand his distinctive language. Such an expectation is either naïveté or arrogance. If I join a community where a tongue other than my own is the medium of intercourse, I simply must learn the language of the place to the best of my ability. Anything less is wrong. The Catholics of our land have not reflected on this truth sufficiently. That non-Catholics do not know more of the Catholic idiom is regrettable, but that the Catholics do not know the language of their non-Catholic milieu is tragic.

Actually there is a movement on foot among the younger

members of the Catholic community to learn and talk fluently the tongue of our environment. Fortunately, they are receiving encouragement from some of the elders who recognize the need and are, in their way, helping to meet it. However, there is yet a difficulty.

I remember that as a boy, my sister and I were forbidden to speak English in our home. There was an advantage in the prohibition. I did not have to learn English where it was badly spoken. But there was a great disadvantage. My sister and I spontaneously spoke English when together. For us, the *Alemanisch* of our household began to stand for something alien and strange which we could indeed use but never did use beyond the ears of our parents. A kind of schizophrenia came over us. For our parents, who were well aware of what was going on, a parallel discomfort was produced. Somehow, their own were not their own.

Something analogous happens in the Catholic community. The oldsters talk their Catholic dialect and insist that the youngsters do likewise. The youngsters, by necessity, learn the language but they are bilingual. They can also speak the general cultural medium of the total community. In fact, among themselves they will prefer to talk it. For many an oldster, this is a kind of apostasy and lack of loyalty. Needless to say, with time this situation will change because of the inevitable death of the oldsters. But in the meantime the youngsters are schizophrenic and troubled by the suggested possibility that they are rejecting something which in reality they deeply cherish.

What makes it difficult for the oldsters is that they simply do not properly understand the language which the youngsters use more correctly. It sounds to them barbaric and ineffective. This reaction induces a hostility to the new. There comes a passionate insistence that the older dialect be used exclusively and a truculence builds up against the newer idiom. Hence, during the period of transition there is malaise.

When I use the word "language" I mean, of course, a jargon configuration and not a linguistic species. The vast majority of Catholics in America now speak English. Bilingualism in the linguistic sense has almost ceased to be a Catholic problem.

The reasons why Catholics remain aloof from some concerns common to their general environment are many. One is the defense mentality which is part of our American Catholic tradition. The Catholic in America had a tough row to hoe. His existence was under attack all through the nineteenth century. I do not refer merely to Know-Nothingism or the Ku Klux Klan. These things were symptomatic of something deeper. Through inner logic and historical circumstances, the Reform tradition was hostile to Catholicism. The first Catholics who came to this land had to face this hostility even though most of its manifestations were neither cruel nor physical. The Catholic was made to feel that he was an intruder, accepted because of the magnanimous sufferance of the masters of the house. The degree of sufferance varied in different communities, but in any community the initially small group of Catholics was greeted with less than wholehearted acceptance.

This situation produced in the Catholics a beleaguered-beachhead mentality. Long after the reaction was logical, it stayed on—even to our day. It may strike the non-Catholic reader as strange, but the average Catholic in this country expects something less than a kind reception at the hands of non-Catholics. Usually this expectation is ungrounded but every now and again it is fulfilled. Hence, the expectation does not die easily.

This situation exists even where visibly there is no real warrant for it. The old American cities like Boston, New York and Philadelphia are today in no sense Protestant com-

munities. In New York the Protestants are really a small
minority, numbering perhaps no more than 20 per cent of
the total, and of this 20 per cent, half are whites and half
colored. Nor do these two halves manifest a tight solidarity.
Yet, even in New York, where the Catholics represent something between 30 and 40 per cent of the population, the defense complex is still at work. It frequently manifests itself
in aggressiveness, which reaction always betrays a feeling
of insecurity rather than tranquil confidence.

This too will pass with time. In fact, it is just as well that
the Catholics at the moment do not realize their numerical
strength. They could easily be tempted to abuse it. In the in-
terim, Catholics and non-Catholics will grow up together,
neither side attacking the other. A perduring precedent of
friendly living together should make future social integra-
tion easy and natural.

If the Catholic has the principal obligation of overcoming
the current impasse of communication in a land culturally
non-Catholic, the non-Catholic has a lesser but not less real
obligation. By and large, the American non-Catholic is eager
to enter into dialogue with the Catholic on a friendly basis.
I do not refer to the secular social relationships where Catholic and non-Catholic have already fused. Almost everyone
has Catholic and non-Catholic friends and relatives. No social aggregation in our vast society is without its representa-
tion of Catholics and non-Catholics. But these social enclaves
prescind from religion. Today, the American non-Catholic
also wants to encounter the American Catholic *qua* Catholic.
This feeling is actually stronger on the non-Catholic than on
the Catholic side. It is certainly a good movement and it
should be aided by all.

However, there is a possible danger in the movement.
Given the latent indifferentism in so many contemporaneous

Protestants, they may receive the Catholic on an indifferentist basis. This basis is a belief that all religious groups are equally good, or putting it reversely, equally bad. No denomination, church or sect is totally bad or totally good. We can all learn from each other and must apologize to each other. Are we not all God's children, going home by different roads? Now this is an impossible approach to the Catholic. He believes, indeed, that all roads lead to God, but only because all roads lead to Rome, which certainly is not the belief of the indifferentist.

This explains a strange phenomenon in our time. In the past the stubborn antagonists of Catholicism were the Bible Christians or fundamentalists as we call them today. When the different forms of liberalism took over in the Reform denominations, this hard resistance lost much of its unyieldingness. Historically, then, the Catholic who by the structure of his faith can never be a Biblicist fundamentalist, should look more kindly on the liberals than on the fundamentalists. Yet the opposite tends to take place. The reason is simple enough. Even though the fundamentalist is traditionally opposed to the Scarlet Woman of Rome and her ways, yet he clings to certain positions which are as fundamental for him as for Catholics. He believes in the divinity of Jesus of Nazareth, the Virgin birth, the objectively atoning death of Jesus and His physical resurrection. The liberals vacillate ambiguously in their adherence to these dogmas. In consequence, the Catholic feels sympathy for the fundamentalist in spite of the latent antipathy felt by that group toward Catholicism. The liberals are far more friendly and more cordial but the Catholic is appalled by their radical reconstructions of Christianity. It is easier and more pleasant to talk to a neoliberal than to a fundamentalist, but there is a greater community of dogmas—for different reasons—in a fundamentalist-Catholic encounter. Tradition is the main

concern of the Catholic and, surprised as the tradition-reject-
ing fundamentalist may be on hearing it, he is more traditional than his neoliberal companion.

But indifferentism is not the only pitfall the Protestant
must avoid in order to help intercommunication with Catholics. A graver and often more unconscious assumption in an
interfaith dialogue can be more deadly. The Catholic today
with no little success is translating his own formulas so that
they can be genuinely understood by those outside his
church. As a result, many a non-Catholic now sees that a
typical Catholic formula is not as silly as he once believed.
He may even see that he himself actually holds what the
genuinely understood Catholic proposition states. A strange
reaction is now possible. Because the non-Catholic sees the
Catholic statement in a new light, he thinks the Catholics
have changed. Actually, the change has been in the non-
Catholic, but he is not sufficiently aware of it. The non-Catholic spontaneously thinks that the Catholics are "reforming";
they are finally coming to their senses. Perhaps with a little
time they will become Protestant, not, of course, in name but
in belief. For the non-Catholic there seem to be many straws
in the wind. He is convinced that Father Leonard Feeney
gave the traditional doctrine of the Catholics on the matter
of the salvation of non-Catholics and he sees therefore a welcome change in the Church's official repudiation of this
doctrine.

Yet the repudiation of Father Feeney's understanding of
the axiom: *Extra ecclesiam nulla salus,* was not based on a
change of doctrine in the Church. The Feeney doctrine was
rejected because it was not traditional. The Roman authorities were not making a concession to Reform-adherents but
judging a Catholic preacher in the light of their inner domestic norms. The perennial Catholic position on the saving
power of God is not to be found in the Boston priest's explanation but in its opposite.

Gradual increase in mutual understanding does not mean that the two parties in the dialogue are tending to become one in belief. Crusts of misunderstanding and antipathy are being pared off a historical division, but the division itself remains. With the greatest of sympathy and comprehension on both sides, we shall still be faced by separation. Protestantism may disappear, though no one seriously thinks that such an event is near. The hypothesis of the end of Catholicism is conceivable, though not by a Catholic. But until one of the two events be realized, there will be a Catholic-Protestant separation. It is foolish to think that the two groups will fuse into some Catholic-Protestant amalgam.

The realistic acceptance of this fundamental truth is necessary for the non-Catholic in his friendly meeting with Catholics. He must not believe that the Catholic will become something else, though remaining a Catholic. The Catholic can drop his allegiance to his Church, but he cannot become a non-Catholic Catholic. If the teleology of the non-Catholic in his approach to the Catholic is to convert him to some other faith, he should not be surprised if his efforts are resented.

Nor is there any need that conversion be the objective of encounter and dialogue. It may be and probably will be the secret hope of both sides, but the hope concerns a possible consequence rather than the purpose to be achieved in coming together. A male is not a female but they can and must live together in harmony with no futile attempt to change the sex of either party. In a pluralistic society, the presence of differences is the fundamental postulate of a human situation. We are socially conjoined to each other no matter how great our lack of complete harmony, and the conjunction can be happy, fruitful and invigorating.

5

✠✠✠

An Introduction to
American Catholicism

✠✠✠

THERE ARE three over-all traits which distinguish American Catholicism from Catholicism elsewhere.

First, Catholicism is not something traditionally inherent in the American way of life. For a Greek Orthodox, to be Greek means to be Orthodox, so that a non-Orthodox Greek is no true Greek. No American at any moment of the life of this country believed that to be American also meant to be Catholic. There have been and there still are many Americans who believe the opposite, namely, that to be American means to be non-Catholic. This position, however, is no longer soundly tenable either in the abstract or in the concrete. Yet it is true that American Catholics have always been a minority in this land; an insignificant minority in the first days of the republic and an important minority in our own time. Hence at no time was the established cultural pattern of America inducive to Catholicism, although the vision of the Constitution effectively made religion an unhampered force for the individual and individual groups.

Moreover, the phenomenal rise of American Catholicism during the last hundred years was caused by the immigration of men and women from different and foreign cultures. Catholicism became definitively American only after 1914, and there are still isolated Catholic groups which have not become thoroughly absorbed into American civilization. Bilingualism is more common in Catholic communities than in their non-Catholic counterparts, though bilingualism is a disappearing problem in Catholic circles.

In consequence of this basic fact, we do not find what is common in Europe where there is the spontaneous tendency to take for granted that the individual member of the civic community is an adherent of the religion of the national culture. Such a spontaneous assumption leads to dangerous misunderstandings. In many so-called Catholic countries, in spite of the supposition that the overwhelming majority is Catholic, the fact is evident that the vast mass is Catholic only in a cultural sense. If they have religion, it will most probably be Catholic, but the majority is not infrequently removed from religion. To substitute population statistics for Church statistics is a woeful error.

The American Catholic has explicitly chosen to be a Catholic. It was not thrust upon him by a culture. It is true that family influences have conditioned his choice, so that we expect certain communities to bring forth only Catholics, yet if the individual wishes to become a Protestant or an indifferentist (as almost half of all Americans are), this is easily possible. No social condemnation will fall upon him. You must always ask the American if he is a Catholic or a non-Catholic; you cannot take it for granted that he is one or the other, no matter what be his background. This explains why so many Catholics have drifted out of the Church. The environment and the history of the land did not exert any pressure because of which they felt compelled to retain a thin, nominal allegiance to Catholicism. It is not uncommon on the American scene to find families with Catholic and non-Catholic branches, although in the beginning they were all either Catholics or non-Catholics.

This explicitly chosen adhesion of American Catholics to their church makes Catholicism a vital thing. It is theirs not only because they once were exposed to it but because they want it here and now. In consequence they make sacrifices for it, because they are by their continuously exercised choice attached to it. The impressive material aspect of American Catholicism has its root in this explicitly willed allegiance to the Church. The thousands of churches, the universities, hospitals and institutions of American Catholics are monuments of the self-sacrifice of all the Catholics. They built all these things in less than a century, not in the course of ten. They built them not with the ample legacies of a few rich men, but with the many pennies of the poor. The generosity of American Catholics for Catholic causes is matched in very few places of the world.

Another consequence of the nonidentification of Catholicism with American culture is the American Catholic's attitude toward religions which are not his own. There are very few Americans who live in a community where all the members belong to the same church. As a result, the American Catholic lives, works and plays with non-Catholics. Intermarriage is an unavoidable characteristic of such a milieu, though in America it is not so frequent as one might spontaneously suppose. Yet religiously there is little contact between American Catholics and non-Catholics. Many a European has a better knowledge of American Protestantism than most American Catholics. Many a European Catholic is scandalized by the small efforts made by American Catholics to attract non-Catholics religiously. The American Catholic has kept quite aloof from non-Catholic religious life, yet nonetheless it is impossible for him to entertain fantastic notions concerning Protestants; he knows too many. He certainly has no ill will for them, and he contributes to their organizations of charity. He cannot conceive of them as the great enemy, although this is the attitude of many Latin Catholics in Europe and Ibero-America. In many instances there is collaboration between Catholic and non-Catholic groups, but this never takes place on the plane of religion itself. The frequent American meetings of a purely civic or quasi-religious nature will bring a Protestant minister, a Jewish rabbi and a Catholic priest together on the platform, each of whom will say a public prayer. However, this phenomenon is essentially cultural, not religious. But the result is that almost all American Catholics have at some time or another bowed their heads in prayer led by non-Catholic clergymen. Likewise Catholic priests and Protestant ministers dress alike in public. It is impossible to distinguish them, though we must not forget that the majority of Protestants do not usually wear the Roman collar. The American Catholic takes religious pluralism as an obvious fact. He is not disedified or scandalized by it. His own love of religion makes him prefer to have his neighbor in some church rather than in no church at all. The general effect is that the American Catholic is much more tolerant of non-Catholic religions than members of European communities where only one religion is effectively present. This tolerance may be interpreted by some superficial observers as a diminished allegiance to Catholicism, though such an interpretation would be very wide of the mark. Catholic tolerance is caused by an exercise of charity rather than by a defect of faith.

The second generalization to help us in our consideration of American Catholicism can be expressed by describing the American Catholic as more activist than contemplative. It is not mere whimsy to say that most American Catholics believe that our Lord was not altogether fair to Martha and too partial to Mary. The American preacher urges his hearer to activity and moral endeavor in a program of concrete works. He does not dwell on dogma which is taught routinely in the synthetic form of the catechism, once and for all. Church for most Americans means something to do rather than something to think about. It is a trait of all Americans to be cold and suspicious of intellectual schemes, especially when they are brilliant pieces of dialectic. Their prime interest is in the practical program attached to a thought scheme. Hence it is logical that the life of an American Catholic parish is a constant whirl of activity, and this explains the greater vitality of the American parish in contrast to the European. The school the Catholic boy attends is in the majority of cases the parish school. The organization to which he belongs is a parish chapter of some national union. His father and mother belong to societies which arrange social meetings in the parish hall. The larger boys form athletic teams on whose uniforms is sewed the name of the parish, and often enough the instructor of the team is one of the parish priests. The constant need of money for parish and diocesan projects brings the Catholics together in all kinds of fund-raising enterprises ranging from simple games of chance to elaborate theatricals. The youth organizations plan and conduct dances sponsored by the religious society to which they belong. Catholic life in America is intensely active, and many of the activities, which of their nature are not religious, have assumed for Catholics a religious meaning. In consequence even their genuinely religious exercises are tinged with this activism. The American Catholic uses language for his religious life which indicates this activism. He is always "going" and "making"; he "goes" to church, he "goes" to communion, he "goes" to confession, he "makes" a retreat.

To many a European this materialistic approach to the

sacred is understood as infantile and anti-intellectualistic. Such a formulation of the facts is misleading. The American, Catholic or non-Catholic, is no opponent of thought. His universities, so many and so lively, produce and communicate thought. However, because of the English roots of his culture, the American judges thought by its practical conclusions rather than by its abstract premises. In doing so, he is only applying the maxim of our Lord who taught that by their fruits you shall know them. That is why the clearest example of American thinking is the disciplined organization he erects for concrete tasks. The organization builds on thought and through thought, with the result that American activity is highly rational. In fact, the American becomes irritated with the lack of rationality of the *modus operandi* of non-Americans. However, in all such organization, abstract principles must cede to efficiency. Thinking is judged by the end product, not by its inner logical consistency. The American has seen that logically perfect systems can be treacherous or even harmful, and he refuses to see the *summum bonum* in mere logical consistency. This is not anti-intellectualism. It is an antiapriority which insists that thinking must enrich life rather than make life submit to the strangling power of "self-evident" abstractions. Hence an American frequently engages in works which are declared to be impossible by some philosophy or some generally assumed principle. He is bold enough to do so because he knows from his own experience that a priori impossibilities are very often a posteriori possibilities. That is why the American considers no traditional scheme or customary pattern of action as sacrosanct. Within a very conservative framework, he is willing and ready to change all the time. This is the American paradox. Without being a revolutionary, the American is always changing in the hope that by experiment through trial and error he will better achieve his traditional goals.

This general attitude is shared by American Catholics. All visitors to this country are struck by the absence of intellectualism in general American Catholic life. It is true that everywhere small but promising groups are now springing up with a hunger for the intellectual, but as yet they have not deeply tinged American Catholicism. It is a known fact that Catholics do not adopt scholarly careers in great numbers, and as a sector of the total community the Catholics fall far below the proportion they should have in scientific pursuits. It is also true that the Catholic universities in general produce very few scientists and scholars. Even in the sacred sciences the American contribution has been slight, in spite of the large numbers of seminaries and seminarians. The American Catholic has for a long time rested content in looking to Europe for the development of philosophy and theology. Only in the last twenty years do we find isolated efforts to work productively in these fields, and the results up to the moment have not been spectacular. Often, too, the best work is done by foreigners who have established themselves in the United States.

It is hard to explain why this is. We cannot explain it by saying that the Catholics are economically hindered. Certainly the general Catholic population belongs to the low-income groups. Yet the generosity of Catholics is such that they will finance any worthy cause. In the smaller Jewish community many poor boys and girls dedicate themselves to scholarship. They find the financial means in the many foundations which exist for this purpose, and these are available to all.

Nor can we lay the whole blame on the Catholic schools. More than half of our Catholic student population studies in non-Catholic universities and colleges, but this group does not produce more scholars than the Catholic-university group.

Perhaps the explanation is to be found in the origins of the Catholic community itself. The Catholics of today are in very large numbers the sons or grandsons of Europeans who came to this country in order to improve their economic and social positions. The importance of having and earning money is thus unconsciously inculcated by the Catholic family. In America, no less than elsewhere, the scholar is not highly remunerated in terms of dollars. In America rather than elsewhere, there is no social prestige attached to the status of a professor or scholar. The doctor, the lawyer, the clergyman, the politician, the businessman are civic idols, and in these guilds the Catholics are prominent. Professors on the other hand are considered to be dreamers and incompetents. Today they are called "egg-heads," quite in accord with a well-known American saying: He who can, does; he who can't, teaches.

Consequently the two values which attracted the first immigrants, Catholic and non-Catholic, were money and social prestige, and both are unlikely to produce scholars. For the Catholics there is an added difficulty. Those elements of Catholic youth with signs of a scholarly vocation were directed to the priestly or religious life. However, though there is no dearth of vocations in America, priests and religious are led by the imperious necessities of concrete Catholic life to become pastors, administrators and organizers. Those who do teach, for reasons of economy have many other occupations or heavy teaching loads and they do not lead truly scholarly lives. They communicate what is commonly accepted without engaging in the labors of productive scholarship.

The general picture is not too pleasant, but there are signs of an awakening to a lack in American Catholic life, and there are younger groups anxious to dedicate themselves to lives of study and contemplation. Only the future can say if they will fulfill their promise, but it is already true today that things intellectual are more highly considered than they were twenty years ago. Books in abundance, readily available to all, plus the felt want of a Catholic intellectualism may perhaps do what the teaching fraternity did not do: create a representative group of Catholic intellectuals.

One consolation the American Catholic draws from his own intellectual poverty is the reflection that it is the price for something valuable (in American eyes, more valuable), the vigorous life of the Church on the level of the nonintellectual. When the American Catholic visits Europe he is delighted and impressed by the flourishing intellectualism of the European churches, but he clearly sees that it affects only a very small group, while the vast masses are lethargic in their realization of Catholic faith. In fact, Catholic intellectuals often take a pharisaic attitude to the "people," considering them quite incapable of true Catholicism. Such an attitude is clearly sterile snobbery produced by a cowardly inability to communicate the gospel to every creature.

The third and last guiding generalization would state that American culture is highly respectful of religion and piety. It is safe to say that nowhere in the world with the possible exception of Ireland is the religious in so high esteem.

This general thesis comes as a surprise to many Europeans who uncritically believe that America is the incarnation of materialism, the land of the Philistine, the proper home of the tawdry and the vulgar. Nothing is further from the truth than this conception of the United States, and it must be flatly said that the man who believes in such an idea is very ignorant. Religion was and is an important factor in American life. We need not defend the dubious opinion of some Catholics who wish to prove that the Constitution was directly derived from religious principles. Many of the founding fathers of the republic were not very religious men, and the notion of God which pleased their leaders was a deistic construction. However, the religious roots of life in America were too strong to permit the authors of the Constitution, even had they so wished, to ignore religion, much less oppose it. From that time on, religion was always a respected phase of American life. It has at times taken bizarre shapes; it has often had little to contribute to the activities of the moment; but it was never attacked. Instead, it has always been given deferential treatment. Of course, individual religions have been persecuted by groups and mobs, but never with the consent of law or in odium of religion itself. The attacks were made because concrete religions were considered unpatriotic or corruptive religions. Anti-Catholicism has constantly made itself visible in America, nor are we surprised when we see it flare up momentarily even in our own time, but this is not an attack on the concept of religion as such. Anti-Semitism is by no means dead in the United States, but it is not dynamized by an opposition to the Jewish faith.

It would be wise to say something here concerning the American separation of Church and State. This famous phrase means one thing to a European and another to an American. The old European liberals used the phrase in a conscious effort to eliminate religion as a force in public life. The phrase meant the reduction of the Church to a place in public law as a social union subject to the government. The liberals were not satisfied with the mere separation of the two things but tried to make the Church subservient to the State, which was turned into a secularistic leviathan, with no morals by which it was to be ruled and with no God to whom it was subject. The old liberal slogan was really the apotheosis of the State. In America this was not so. The Declaration of Independence begins with a profession of faith in God as the creator of all men, and the first article of the Bill of

Rights attached to the Constitution prevents the State from any interference with religion and the free exercise thereof. The whole function of the Constitution is to restrict the powers of government and to arrange things so that the State would never be apotheosized. To this day the American tradition has ever been to suspect government in order to keep it a pliant instrument of the people rather than to have it be their lord. In the Constitution the people put religion beyond the State, not the State beyond religion.

From the first moment of the application of the Constitution to American life we find this understanding clearly made manifest. The Congress had its chaplains, and so did the troops of the nation. The churches were exempt from taxes and clergymen exempt from any military duties other than spiritual. Religious marriage was recognized as civically valid, and in many states it was the only recognized form of marriage. Public officials entered into their offices by taking an oath on the Bible. All the Presidents once a year proclaimed one day to be set aside in order to give thanks to God for favors received. The State was under religion but religion itself was beyond governmental power. The Constitution could only speak of religion in general, because no single church of the many in the land represented the religion of the citizens as a whole. The constitutional separation of Church and State was made to assure the liberty of the Church, not its exile from public life. Politicians and statesmen from the beginning until now have always been sensitive to religious opinion. Nor has there ever been a movement hostile to faith. Religion is presumed to have a right to criticize the government, and such criticism is never rejected as impertinent. It is not false to say that the churches are the conscience of the nation, and the government is the instrument of a nation with a conscience. Where the churches agree, the government will obey—but agreement is very difficult where two hundred and fifty different churches exist.

This spirit pervades not only political life but also social life as a whole. A man's faith is sacred and must be respected by his fellows. The American stage, screen and press carefully respect religious conviction and religious symbols. The rare jests about clergymen are always kindly, and more a sign of friendship than hostility or contempt. It is a general presumption that a man believes in God, and has some religious connection, even if only desultory and informal. The clergy are really a privileged class. They travel on the nation's railroads (all of which are private) with a 50 per cent reduction of fares. Very many shops and business houses will give them rebates on their purchases. They will be treated by doctors for little or no fee. When queues are formed in restaurants or public gatherings, the clergy are usually escorted to places without awaiting their turn. No nun will ever have to stand in a crowded bus or train; from all sides men and women will offer her a seat. (This great deference to the clergy is certainly one element in the explanation of the large numbers of American vocations to the priesthood and the religious life.)

In such an environment piety can evolve freely. In the American Catholic Church it has evolved, but it has taken on the modality of the culture of the land. Now the American has a horror of manifesting deep emotions of a personal kind. Piety is considered as primarily personal, and hence it is presumed to be in bad taste to flaunt it in public or even to discuss it. This does not imply any shame because of personal piety or faith, but rather a respect for the holy. A constant reference to one's own or another's religion is considered vulgar and ill-bred. According to American mores religion should not appear in the market place, not because the market place is not subject to religion, but because it is not dignified enough to house the religious. The colorful public processions of Mediterranean Catholics are not forbidden by American law: they simply grate on American sensitivity.

Because of the limiting action of American culture, American Catholic piety is peculiar. No visitor to this land is left unimpressed with a visit to a metropolitan church in the busier parts of the cities. Day and night, at all hours, he will find Catholic worshipers at prayer in silence and devotion. The very silence of the church is a living silence, not the silence of an empty tomb. If a visitor attends a Catholic service he will again be impressed by the mannerly conduct of the people. There are no wanderers gadding about; no youths standing at the church door eying the girls who enter; no chattering or conversation. If the visitor comes from certain countries, he is surprised at seeing almost as many men as women present in the pews as well as at the communion rail. But the same visitor will be shocked to find a collector at a table at the church door demanding an entrance fee. (It really is not a universal custom nor is it an "entrance fee.") He will also be surprised that confessions should be heard only on Saturday afternoons and evenings, but the American Catholics have been disciplined so that they will go to confession only on that day, and they will go in large numbers. In general the visitor will be pleased with the decency of the churches, some of which are extremely beautiful.

In spite of the fact that American Catholicism is chiefly metropolitan and numerically weak in rural areas, Sunday Mass attendance is very high in comparison with that of most European countries. Exaggerated statistics are sometimes given, but it is not an imprudent conjecture to suppose that about 50 per cent of the Catholic population assist regularly at Sunday Mass. The Friday abstinence will be observed by the vast majority of Catholics, so that all American restaurants have special meatless menus for that day. The last Catholic custom which the man drifting out of the Church will relinquish will be Friday abstinence. Only when he has considered himself definitively out of the Church will he begin to eat meat on Fridays.

But the European visitor who sees all these things: the many communions, the frequent confessions, the impressive attendance at Sunday Mass, will say that these are only externals. What is the state of mind in the Catholics who do all these things? The visitor probably is thinking of intellectualism, and since this is generally absent in American piety, he will find American devotion childish. He will be confirmed in his opinion when he sees the popularity of the nonliturgical novena devotions held everywhere and often with a commercial aspect of miracle-mongering. If he reads the typical diocesan weekly paper, he will note a saddening mediocrity of content and a mass appeal in its format. Many a visitor goes away with the conviction that the American church attendance is merely mechanical with no inner force.

Such a conviction can bring evidence in its favor, but it is not justified by the total reality it is judging. In the first place, it is certainly better that our Catholics go to Mass rather than stay away. The material element is the first desideratum, even if not the whole demand. Secondly, the Catholic American is not mechanically present in his pew. He is exercising his piety. The piety of the American Catholic is childlike but not at all childish. It does not rest on profound theology but on deep faith, faith not rationally understood but highly cherished. One might superficially accept the statement that the American Catholics are not convinced Catholics but they are thoroughly persuaded Catholics. The first tie the Catholic feels to the Church is the bond of loyalty. Very many go to Mass not because it involves any religious experience or because of the excellence of the sermons (which are all too frequently far from excellent), but out of loyalty. This loyalty also explains his readiness to answer the

appeals of his pastors and bishops with alacrity and effect.
The peculiarly American virtue of "team spirit" (which is
more than *esprit de corps*), can be found in the Catholic even
in his religious life and in his piety. In American Catholics
there is a strong persuasion that the team must not fail, and
if for some reason or other one member of the team falters
in his task, another will jump into his place spontaneously.
Within the team obedience is always predominant. Orders
are not criticized or analyzed; they are fulfilled. The criticism comes afterward, especially if the effort was not successful.

There are, however, two consequences of the American
mode of Catholic piety which can be disturbing. Its essential
notes are a closed interiority for individual piety and group
solidarity for external piety. Inviolable interiority brings
with it two bad results. It need not be directed and, in some
sense, it should not be directed. Hence fantastic and unsound
outlooks can be engendered which can easily vitiate the religious life of the individual. Even when this does not take
place, especially in those whose capacity for piety is low, no
external manifestation is in theory permitted. This accounts
in great part for the indistinguishability of the Catholic in
the ordinary activities of life. In the office, in the factory, in
the professions, and in social intercourse, the Catholic is
rarely distinguished from his non-Catholic fellows. The behavior of both is the same. It is not rare for a Catholic to discover only after years of friendly relations that the man who
works next to him is a Catholic also. This is inevitable, for
piety should not be manifested and it is impolite to talk
about it. What is worse, many Catholics, though quite strict
in matters of domestic morality, Catholics who see to it that
their children are solidly grounded in ethical matters by giving a splendid example themselves, will in professional life
be unscrupulous and sophistic in their evasions of public

morality. Not a few Catholic figures in public life have been convicted of highly immoral action, though their sincere and devout adhesion to Catholicism was indisputably evident. The moral shortcomings of the total American community are shared by the Catholics with no notable resistance. The Catholic has striven so hard and so long to be accepted by the American community that he has taken on the color and habits of the general environment, keeping his piety well out of sight. Now that he is unquestionably accepted, he is very loath to do anything which would isolate him from his group, which in its outlook is not Catholic. Piety is invisible and conformity is visible. The American Catholic's attempt at adaptation to his milieu has been successful, perhaps too successful.

Besides the indistinguishability of the Catholic from the non-Catholic, we have the second ambiguity in American Catholicism. The loyal solidarity of the faithful is inspiring, but it entails a lack of sense of responsibility in the formation of programs of activity. The inauguration of projects and their direction are largely left to the clergy. The role of the clergy in American Catholic life is immense. Obviously it should be so in matters of faith, morals and sacramental life. Yet the clergy are dominant beyond these fields. One would imagine such a dominance would arouse anticlericalism. But it does not. The reasons are many, but all are derived from the American Catholic situation. First of all, the priest is not removed from the people and in his own being and evolution he is rooted in his community. American Catholicism is in general lower middle class tapering upward, and so are the priests. As an American bishop said publicly, not one American bishop can point to a father who had a college degree. This dictum may not be totally exact, but it certainly is true of the majority of bishops and priests. Priests who come from the laboring class remain loyal to that class and in their priestly activities in the field of labor problems, they represent the laborers' point of view rather than the position of management. Because there is an identity between the priest and the people, he is welcome in all the affairs of his parishioners. His priestly prestige is no obstacle to his sharing in the total life of his congregation. He plays golf, he bowls, he jokes and jests, he sits at the family table. The people are glad to have him around, and youth welcomes him enthusiastically.

The Americans are also strict believers in the distribution of labor. It seems, in consequence, natural that the priest, one of the people, should lead the religious activities of the people. The people expect it and want it so, for, strangely enough, American life in work and play trains them for it. Perhaps American play brings this out best. Non-Americans are often amazed to see how mechanical an American sports event can be. The players are instructed in every detail, and they are expected to obey these instructions. There is little room for spontaneous and personal initiative. The game moves according to a plan fathered and developed not by the players but by the coach. Would it be altogether wrong to say that great sports competitions in this country are struggles between two invisible coaches rather than between two visible teams? One cannot say "no" without reserve, and something of this spirit permeates all American activity.

Hence it is not surprising that it works in American Catholicism as well. The modalities of older, European-born pastors who successfully ran their parishes like benevolent despots are no longer popular today and they are a sign of the past. But the modern American pastor does something similar but in a genuinely American fashion. He does not order like a king; he orders like a coach. He is of the people but he is a specialist, and as such he has the freely granted right to lead. If he invokes authority, he is lost; if he appeals to his competence as a specialist, he is a success.

No matter how we explain it, it still remains true that the clergy are all too prone to keep the laity out of tasks of planning, and the laity are only too pliant to accept planning and the competent knowledge for it as the reserve of the priests. There is an energetic passivity in American Catholics, but they are weak in initiative.

These three generalizations (for they are not universally valid) will help to give an objective picture of American Catholicism. I repeat the generalizations: first, Catholicism is not induced by American culture but is the exercised choice of the American Catholics; second, the American Catholic is activist rather than contemplative; third, America is propitious to religion and piety so that Catholicism has had a splendid opportunity to develop its own life, which it did in an American way.

In the light of these synthetic generalizations the American Catholic fact can take on significance. The brute fact is obvious enough and quite impressive. In America, of a total population of more than 170,000,000, there are 36,000,000 Catholics. This figure is much more realistic than the usual calculations for the countries which culturally are Catholic. The vitality of this church is suggested by its statistics. Within the American Church we have 4 cardinals, 31 archbishops, 190 bishops, 138 dioceses (three of which are of the Byzantine rite), 50,813 priests, 9,694 brothers, 164,575 nuns, 16,552 parishes, 20 universities and 230 university colleges, 516 seminaries, 2,434 secondary schools, 10,159 elementary schools, 939 hospitals, 609 asylums.[1] It is to be remembered

[1] These round numbers are based on the statistics published in *The Official Catholic Directory. A.D. 1958* (New York: Kenedy & Sons, 1958).

that financial resources for the economic maintenance of this vast structure come exclusively from the free-will offerings of the faithful. The government contributes nothing to their support.

We must not fall into the error, pardonable in adolescents and adolescent nations, of considering large numbers as indicators of large significance. Quality is always more meaningful than mere quantity. However, quantity itself is not meaningless. It must be judged in the light of its qualitative significance.

6

✠✠✠

Catholic and Protestant
Theologies in Outline

✠✠✠

It is becoming embarrassing to be a theologian, because everywhere people are talking religion and compelling anyone who has studied divinity to answer every type of question. The Protestant theologian must know not only his own theology but Catholic theology as well, and the same is true for the Catholic. It is very difficult for one man to know even superficially all the theology of his own tradition, and all but impossible to know intimately and sympathetically the theologies of the other traditions. To keep up comprehensively with all the theological work done in the four corners of the globe is simply out of the question. Yet, in spite of these difficulties, a bird's-eye view of contemporaneous Catholic and Protestant theologies can be offered to the layman who wishes to know "what it is all about."

The Catholic theological tradition is not a series of historically contiguous but different theologies; it is a continuous effort in a uniform line. A twentieth century theologian can go back to the thirteenth or sixteenth century and not be in an unknown, strange world. He is quite at home, because it is the very house he is living in today. Certain necessary remodeling jobs have been done and certain additions have been made, but it is still the same edifice, the old rooms are still lived in. There is central heating now and electricity, but the fireplaces have not been removed. There are elevators, but the magnificent stairs of the older time are still there. Even the moat can still be seen, though today it is used for flower beds, and the drawbridge is always down.

The original builders were concerned with doing a solid piece of work. The modern builders see that it was a solid job, more solid than they singlehandedly can do today. Hence, they keep the old and add organically those parts which are needed to make the house serve in our time and for which allowance had been made by the original builders. Plenty of room was left for the successors, and the ground plan was drawn to permit new developments which could not be foreseen in their time.

The Protestant theological house does not follow such a plan; it is really a rambling complex of buildings. At any moment it obeys the dictates of the tastes of the time, but one can see in the whole that there were once other structures where present ones now stand. The older parts have been torn down, though elements thereof were employed in the present erections. If you examine the rock gardens about the edifice, you will see that they are actually the ruins of earlier buildings, gently enhanced today with flowers, although they serve no functional purpose. If we look closely, we shall also see that the original lines of the house have been changed. The building does not face precisely as it did in the beginning. Looking over the grounds, we can see that some parts of the old building were burned down in a conflagration.

Let me explain the parable. Protestant theology is a function of Protestant religion. That is obvious enough, but it necessarily brings with it consequences which are not so obvious. Many Protestants and Catholics have considered Protestantism as a highly individualistic religious vision. However, in our time we all see that this description of Protestantism is misleading. Protestantism from its onset is now seen to have been intensely communal by desire and theory.

What distinguished the Catholic community from the Protestant community was the fact that for the Protestant, in principle, there was no final authority in the community. Over, above, and outside the community floated the Bible. Its authority was originally considered final, but the community, on principle, had no authority to define its meaning. The fellowship necessarily had the power to exclude members who did not conform to the total community's interpretation, but it had no structural norm whereby another understanding could definitely be declared invalid. In practice it tried to do so, but the nuclear principle of Protestantism contradicted the practice. As a result, the fragmentation of Protestantism was inevitable. With the same right that the first reformers claimed to reform the actual Church in the light of their sincere understanding of the Bible, new reformers within the Protestant community again reformed the Church in the light of their sincere understanding of revelation. This process by inner logic has continued until our own time. But no matter how often the fragmentation took place, it never gave final authority to the community; and with this lack, future fragmentation could not be avoided. The World Council of Churches is a most interesting phenomenon because it is the modern Protestant's impressive attempt to overcome the inner drive to fragmentation.

In the light of this basic fact in Protestantism, Protestant theology cannot follow the Catholic norm of theology which is the definitive teaching of the living Church. In the beginning, the only Protestant norm was the Scripture understood in the light of the infant philology of the sixteenth century. This could produce a Biblical theology, but logically it could give no system. Yet, one of the most important products of the early reform was Calvin's *Institutes of the Christian Religion,* a perfect model of system.

It is interesting to see how Calvin formed his synthesis. As an outline he followed the non-Biblical Apostles' Creed. His methodological postulates were as follows: the inerrancy of Scripture; the luminosity of the Bible to the faith-enlightened; the basic reliability of the theology of the early Church, though this reliability was not universal or absolute. In the light of these postulates he could teach the doctrine of salvation by confident trust alone; the total and abiding sinfulness of man, incapacitating him for just action; the divine overlooking of this incapacity through grace, not only freely but immediately given by God in obedience to the free predestination of some men to salvation. He introduced one important negative concept: the Church did not sanctify its members, but rather was a community of those who were immediately sanctified by God. Consequently the Church's action was not productive of grace through her sacraments but only the occasion whereby God inspired trust in the predestined. The Church was merely the custodian of the Bible and the ingathering for the trusting elect.

In this system the formal and material elements are not immediately Scriptural. They are largely Augustinian, and Calvin had a conscious affection for Augustine. By his postulate that the early Church was, by and large, reliable in her theology, he could take as much of Augustine as he wanted without being forced to take it all. He could always stop Augustine by an ultimate appeal to Scripture. What he did take from Augustine he could justify by claiming to see it in the Scripture. However, as it was evident to him and to others, the Scriptures were understood differently by other reformers, the Lutherans and the Anabaptists, for example. He lamented this difference, but he found a basic unity in the Protestant positions inasmuch as they all made the Scripture the only final authority, thus opposing themselves to Rome, which made its teaching the final norm.

The eighteenth century changed all that. Rationalism, Kantianism and Romanticism all supplied major premises from which the Biblical affirmations could be dialecticized into conclusions utterly different from those derived in the previous two centuries. The nineteenth century gave the world historicism and Hegelianism, and these in their turn brought out new formulations of theological doctrine. By the twentieth century, liberalism—naturalistic, ethicist, and optimistic—deduced from the Scriptures theological positions quite alien to the theology of the reformers. The First World War ended that phase, and Karl Barth successfully urged a return to the content of the Bible as the revelation of a transcendental God. However, he used as his interpreting philosophy an existentialism manifested in Kierkegaard and developed by Scheler and Heidegger.

All these theologies in some way or other are Biblical. However, except for the fundamentalists, the Bible does not occupy the sole or even main place. Other sources of data are recognized, such as the beliefs of the churches, personal experience, or the findings of science.

It might be of value to point out some questions which today are of interest to the theologians of all schools. The first interest beyond a doubt is the question of the Church. The nature and role of the Church are being studied with depth and anxiety by all modern theologians. The Catholics are no longer exclusively engrossed in the juridical framework of the Church, and they are stressing the supernatural, spiritual reality of Catholicism. Quite germane to this work was the new examination of the relations of the Church to the State. This has been going on now for about fifteen years.

On the Protestant side the interest in the Church stems from the ecumenical movement which began some fifty years ago and in 1948 finally flowered into the World Council of Churches. Both at Amsterdam, which was the first meeting place of the Council, and subsequently at Lund, where in 1952 its subsidiary Commission on Faith and Order met, voices from all over the Christian world gave their opinions and ideas.

It is difficult, if not impossible, for Protestants to achieve a detailed consensus because there is no final authority in the whole gamut of churches, not even in any one church. Consequently, the views run from extreme to extreme. Extreme liberals think that "the Church" is a label to collectivize the churches, which would include the synagogues as well as the Christian tabernacles. They give no more value to the churches than they give to other communities. They are for them voluntary associations freely entered into and freely constructed according to the wishes of the members who compose them. There is nothing holy about a church, although it is a good thing—provided the group keeps out of the secular field and represents the most liberating tendency in a forward-looking society.

The fundamentalists still cling more or less to the notions of the reformers. The visible Church is a community which is the custodian and expositor of the Bible. Hence, the Church is a people of the Book, a fellowship of those who are enlightened and saved by the Scripture. They will admit that there is also a larger view of the Church in which the Church is an invisible union of those who confidently trust in God because of the work of Jesus. This union is very holy because it is made up only of the living saints united with Christ.

However, the union, though present in the world, acts only invisibly, mysteriously, and without any conjoint plan or effort of the members who do not even know each other.

Between these extremes we have the position reached or approached by most of the other Protestant theologians. They recognize that the Church is more than a voluntary society of ethically minded men. They see that the Church is not a flowering of the Bible into a society, but rather that the Bible itself is a flower of the Church. It is not the Bible which carries the Church, but the Church which carries the Bible. The holy community is the carrier of revelation, but they still hold that its normative expression is the Bible. The Church of itself is holy because of its mission, but unfortunately it is very human. In consequence, it exists in a state of hostile division. Not one of the churches is the Church, though all are of it. Not one of the bodies nor yet all together have lived up to their high vocation. The Church as she is in history is not only a sinful but even a sinning Church. This doctrine came out quite clearly in the 1954 meeting of the World Council at Evanston.

The Church-State problem has different dimensions for the Protestant and for the Catholic. For the Catholics the thorny and annoying question is whether Catholic doctrine includes the affirmation of the necessity of the legal establishment of Catholicism in any community whatever its religious constituency. The problem is abstract and in the order of ideal principle because it is obvious to all in the debate that establishment in a religiously pluralistic community is, in practice, out of the question. For the Protestants there is no real problem because, by and large, they deplore legal establishment on principle even where it exists in practice.

For the Protestants the question is not Church versus State, but rather the relation of Christianity to the secular. Here the question is vital. There are all kinds of solutions offered. Karl Barth considers the secular order as existing under the dominion of sin and for the punishment of sin. The Christian cannot avoid being in it, but he should not be of it. The Swiss theologian is not only cool but even hostile to an organized Christian opposition to communism. An extremely opposed position is that of Dr. Charles Lowry of Washington, who has founded a movement to unite believers of all churches to combat communism on religious grounds. An intermediate position would be that of Reinhold Niebuhr, who does not hesitate to pass adverse judgment on communism in the light of Christian doctrine, but who promptly adds that campaigns against it are morally ambiguous because selfish as well as godly motives are involved. For him Christianity necessarily is against communism, but Christians *de facto* will inevitably oppose it for unworthy motives and in the defense of some partial evil. Niebuhr will not urge Christians to Barthian indifference in the matter, but he warns them that they must not be self-righteous in their opposition because it is shot through with human sinfulness.

The Niebuhrian position is the logical consequence of the Protestant theology on nature and grace. This greater issue is the main theological concern of modern Protestant divines. Can Christianity offer salvation to man in terms of the natural powers of humanity? The old-fashioned liberals, who are by no means mere fossil survivors of the past, give an enthusiastic affirmative to the question. Christianity for them is nothing but an efficient mobilization of human powers to bring about the Kingdom of God.

Against this kind of naturalistic optimism the nonnaturalists, like Barth, Brunner, Niebuhr and Tillich, have successfully made war. Old-fashioned liberalism is not the prevailing mood in Protestant theology today. However, we must make it quite clear that the new supernaturalism is a

reform of liberalism and not a return to the thorough supernaturalism of former times. Bultmann, Niebuhr and Tillich
have no patience with the miraculous, Biblical inerrancy, the
literal divinity of Jesus, His resurrection as a physical event,
or a final resurrection of the flesh. Supernaturalism in the
sense of negation of the universal uniformity of the natural
order of process is no more congenial to them than it is to
the unreformed liberals. They merely insist that God is not
in man, though man is under the judgment of God, of whom
we can say nothing valid except through symbolic expression.

An essay at a simplified sketch for this doctrine might take
the following form: Man's anxious recognition of his own
ephemeral existence, which is always threatened by nothingness, brings him up against the imperious, onward élan at
the very heart of all existence. This center cannot be explained according to the categories of finity which describe
only the events of nature. This mystery is the ground of
being, the absolute, the unconditioned, the no-thing to
which all things must be referred ultimately. It is, of course,
the answer to man's ultimate concern; and that is what we
mean by God. It is not reached by meeting or measuring the
finite order, which we reduce to intelligibility as finite forms
of power rendered rational through the use of categories.
The natural order moves in the direction of finite ends, utterly indifferent to the cries of man who is pushed onward
through a deeper impulse of existence which drives him and
all other things as well.

The self-revelation of Being can be occasioned by nature,
history or the Bible—which is a human witness and a pointer
to the revealing God. God does not enter history in any finite
form, such as the Bible or any other historical phenomenon
must be. He is the ground of being, the *prius* of all history
and the term beyond history.

But the supreme and final revelation of God is in Jesus as the Christ. This must not mean that the man Jesus of Nazareth is the revelation, but his life established a *kairos* (opportune moment) wherein the revelation was seen. In this *kairos* the Christ was made manifest. This means that in the vision of those who encountered God because of Jesus, we see the true human answer to the demands of the unconditioned ground of being. There is a total self-surrender to the Lord God in the complete abandonment of all that means self. This is the Pauline *agape* (love) of which Niebuhr speaks and concerning which Nygrén wrote so well. The man of *agape* is in Christ. He is a new being. He is risen above the futilities and meannesses of finite existence, including his own. The trusting self-surrender of man to God in *agape* is faith, and this alone saves man. Salvation, of course, is not the heaven or hell of the older traditions except symbolically. Salvation is the finding of meaning for existence in the light of the transhistorical.

Reinhold Niebuhr's contribution to such thought is his insistence on the sinfulness of man. The Scriptural emphasis on man's perversity is the central emphasis in the theology of Niebuhr. It ultimately means that man in all his actions obeys drives of selfishness manifested by pride and sensuality. Man cannot elude this inescapable condition. This is the true original sin. However, by trust in God, existentially achieved, these sins need not be the source of hopelessness or nausea. In a whole-souled *agape* founded in confidential trust, man, whose actions always remain morally ambiguous, lives his existence meaningfully in Christ. He is *simul justus et peccator* (paradoxically, at once justified and sinful).

The Catholic position on this same question is different. As Catholic theology sees it, man has a supernatural destiny which means much more than a transhistorical justification. Thus man is a fallen man because of the original sin, an event which inaugurated present history. He is not fallen because he is finite, for finitude of itself only made human sin possible, not inevitable. As a remedy against the fatal virus of original sin, physical though spiritual grace is given to man by God, thanks to the merits of Christ. The justified man, who becomes so by entering into the Body of Christ, which is the Church, can now live a godly life. It is true that he has not totally escaped the vitiating influence of the primal Fall, which is still vestigially present as a proneness to evil, but the influence of this native drag downward is no longer dominant. Man's intellect is still darkened and his will weakened, but the darkness and infirmity are overcome substantially by grace, freely given and freely received. Grave sin is still possible and some lesser degree of sinfulness unavoidable, but on the condition of man's love and contrition these two are objectively wiped away by the loving God.

Because of this rejection of inevitable ungodliness, the justified Christian is not *simul justus et peccator,* but rather *ex injusto fit justus* (out of a sinner a just man is made). A Christian humanism is now logically possible. It is true that man cannot construct the Kingdom of God, but man belongs to the world and by divinized action in the world carries out the hidden design of God in the preparation of history for Christ's second coming, which will usher in the final Kingdom. That will end natural history and begin an endless supernatural epilogue concerning which eye has not seen nor ear heard what God has prepared for them who love Him.

Therefore, because of his renewed moral and intellectual strength through the indwelling grace of God, even though sin still mars man's life, he can and must work justice in the world. He cannot flee the trials of time but in faith and love meets them, not only in terms of individualistic self-perfection, but also socially, for society is under God no less than the individual. Man has no right to expect that any of his conceived projects, holy and noble though they be, must achieve actualization, because the path of history has been invisibly traced by the hidden God. Yet, he must do what Christ's example calls for and leave the outcome to the Lord of history, who will make it sing his glory. History unwittingly evolves itself, not "ever onward and upward," but in accord with God's inscrutable ends which certainly contain the eschatological salvation of those who love Him.

In this way the justified man is not only free but really obliged to take part in all the activity of humanity—economics, politics, art, science, philosophy and religion—for all these things are in the world and the world is for Christ. The Prince of this World is ever the enemy of Christ, and he will not be crushed until Christ defeats him definitively; but in the meantime the Christian, whose battle is with powers and principalities, fights the Prince of this World precisely because the Christian is in Christ. He is not confused in battle because of the ambiguity of his actions, for that ambiguity cannot destroy the substantial nobility of his action in Christ. This is why the Christian will take a stand without fear. In him there is the inspiration of Christ and the power of the All-High which will lead him along right ways even unto the Mountain of God. For the deficiencies in his movement onward, the Christian begs God's forgiveness, but he does not need to doubt about the essential rectitude of his way, for he is visibly led by Christ living with man in the Church. He can and always will doubt his own performance of his task, but the task itself is not subject to doubt, no matter what comes of it. In Christ Jesus the Christian has already overcome the world. In hope and not in vision the Christian moves on, for his action is based on intellectual faith which has the force of a convincing argument for what he does not see.

7

***

Protestant Theological
Positions Today

***

THE MEETING of Catholic and Protestant thought always manifests the completely different approaches toward Christianity orientating Catholic and Protestant thinking. Both parties know the same facts and both show the same dedication to Christianity but it means fundamentally different things to the two groups. At the bottom of the diversity lie different conceptions of Christian truth. Protestantism has never been able to make up its mind on what truth is. For some Protestants it is something that was. For others it is something that will be. For the Catholic it is simply something that is. Protestantism has always stressed the flux in reality and Catholicism has always stressed the permanent. From the days of Luther, the Protestant preoccupation has been with the reformation of Christianity either by looking back or by looking forward, and this is essentially the production of a church. For the Catholics the anxiety is the vital conformation of Christian life according to Christ's abiding and unchanging truth presented by the actual Church of today, and this means the conservation of the Church.

Filled with the Protestant preoccupation, an important book appeared in 1950 under the title, *Responsible Christianity*.[1] The author, Justin Wroe Nixon, is a member of the Colgate-Rochester Divinity School. As a thinker he shows comprehension, sincerity and penetration. As a man he manifests a gentle love for all men and an ardent desire to have mankind enjoy the best there is. He will have no foes; he wants only friends. His book presented itself as a kindly but urgent protest against the present mind which he calls naturalism in accord with the label which the representatives of this kind of thinking have chosen for themselves; others would call it the new materialism, the new paganism, secularism, scientism, or simply positivism. Nixon's task, necessary beyond doubt, was undertaken with some reluctance. He put it very well in the following words:

American Christianity today is engaged in a struggle on two fronts. To Christians who have received their higher education in the first quarter of this century it has long been apparent that a vital Christianity has to struggle with the past. It has come as something of a shock to many Christians engaged in this struggle with the past to find that they now have a struggle on another front—with the present. For it is the present they have championed.[2]

Dr. Nixon's words referred to American Protestant theology, but they are also applicable to European Protestant thought. It was a stunned Protestant theology that gradually became conscious of the fact that today, more than ever before in the history of Christianity, the struggle was not with the past but with the present. It was an unpleasant experience, for the Protestant was always of his time, and in the past was one of the principal molders of the then present

---

[1] Justin Wroe Nixon, *Responsible Christianity* (New York: Harper & Brothers, 1950).
[2] *Op. cit.,* Introduction, p. 11.

mood. Now he finds that he cannot go along with the present in its concrete plans for shaping the future. The Protestant theologian suddenly has found himself in a new role: he is no longer desirous of reforming radically an existing order; he now defends it. The novelty of the situation has been embarrassing.

One of the effects of the changed attitude was the necessity of a re-evaluation of Catholicism. In what was once considered the Catholic's unreasonable intransigence, there is now seen a legitimate defense of Christian truth. The result is a new cordiality for Catholic thinking, which the Catholics themselves have been slow to recognize and with which they have not as yet been very eager to correspond. The Catholic's frigidity is regretted by his Protestant confreres and by not a few Catholics, but there is a psychological explanation for it that frequently escapes Protestants. It is not caused by a Roman ukase against collaboration, for Rome has made it quite clear that a common defense against modern materialism is needed and she is not opposed to collaboration for this end. The real cause of Catholic wariness derives from the fact that when engaged in collaboration he is inclined to feel two irritants. First of all, the Protestant struggle with the past was usually a fight with Catholicism either as a Church or as a doctrine. The Catholic has felt himself to be the enemy so long that it is hard for him to realize suddenly that he is now a friend. Secondly, though the Protestant theologian realizes clearly that he has on his hands a struggle with the present, in which struggle the Catholic is a sincerely welcome ally, yet he cannot forget that he also has a struggle with the past, which engenders Protestant discomfort, because his ally for the present is also the enemy from the past.

This was rather patent in the position of Protestant theologians when confronted with Paul Blanshard's *Amer-*

ican Freedom and Catholic Power. The points in Catholicism attacked in that book needed attacking according to Protestant thought, but Blanshard's point of view was secularist and therefore as alien to Protestantism as it was to Catholicism. The result was that most Protestant theologians were forced to do some agile balancing so as not to agree with Blanshard and yet welcome his criticisms of the Catholic Church.[3] As thinking Protestants saw, the Catholic Church was bearing the brunt of an attack which in principle could easily be diverted toward the Protestants themselves.

Most Protestants enthusiastically accept the alliance with Catholics against secularism but they have an unspoken confidence that as a result of "getting together" the Catholics will drop some of their commitments which make them the prolongation of the ancient enemy. When this confidence is thwarted by the Catholic's lack of desire to drop the old doctrines, the Protestant feels hurt and annoyed. This is especially evident in the English reaction to the definition of the doctrine of the Assumption of Our Lady. This has been a tranquil belief among Catholics for many centuries, and there has been no opposition to the doctrine within Catholic theological circles. The definition will change nothing in Catholic thought and piety. Hence the Archbishop of Canterbury defended no Catholic minority in his opposition to the definition but he only voiced the silent fear of so many Protestants who are earnestly looking for collaboration with Catholics against the new materialism, when he said that the Catholic definition hinders cooperation. It is hard to see why it should, unless the ulterior hope of collaboration with the Catholics is to make them drop or cover over with silence Catholic beliefs unpleasant to Protestants. A conjoint effort will not be possible on the basis of the compromise principle:

[3] Cf., e.g., Georges A. Barrois' review of Blanshard's work, *Theology Today,* VI (1950), 561–563.

we'll take back so much and you'll take back so much. Many Catholics feel, rightly or wrongly, that they are invited to collaborate on an unconscious compromise platform, and they have no intention or desire to be in such a position. The difficulty of uniting forces is not entirely on the side of arrogant Catholic intransigence, for even Protestant transigence can be intransigent. Nevertheless, collaboration is absolutely necessary in our time, but it will have to be worked out awkwardly and by salving wounds, real or imaginary, on both sides.

The Protestant recognition of the anti-Christian structure of the modern mind has never been so clearly or so forcefully put as in Dr. Nixon's book. The first chapter, "Our Changed Spiritual Climate," should be read by everyone who is interested in understanding the time in which we live. Dr. Nixon is familiar with the thought of all the speakers for the modern vision of reality. He interprets them as kindly as is humanly possible, but he brings out clearly that their ultimate message is: man is an animal, substantially like other animals, struggling to adjust himself to a world which makes itself important to him only in as far as it favors or thwarts the desires that well up from his inscrutable depths; which is known to him exclusively in the impact it makes on his experience; which spawned him without desire and will shortly swallow him up with no regret. Dr. Nixon is rightly concerned about the future of our civilization if this philosophy sweeps away the religious heritage of the past. By this new vision man is without dignity or significance, and freedom, that imperiled value, will surely disappear.

Dr. Nixon proposes a vision which he considers healthier. It is the vision of Christianity, but a Christianity congenial to our time. He is engaged, like all good Protestants, in church building. With the divining rod of his own religious experience, conditioned in part by the liberal and critical theology of the past century, he moves over the Hebrew-Christian field and pulls out four rocks: the biblical God, a moral law related to Him, a holy community, and a divinely ordained destiny. On these four stones, mortared together with the thought of Jesus, he will build his church whose concrete structure will rise in obedience to the needs of time and place. It is his belief and hope that it will be an acceptable and sturdy shelter for man.

Not all Protestants will be enthusiastic over Dr. Nixon's future church. The more conservative Protestant theologians think that the Reformers' building will do very well. The Princeton Presbyterian group is publishing works dedicated to the notion that Christianity is more than a field of stones to be collected by a church builder. It is the opinion of this group that Christianity is a structure which cannot be changed without losing its right to be called Christian. Among the works published by this circle is a volume of Benjamin Breckinridge Warfield's Christological studies gathered together by Samuel C. Craig under the title *The Person and Work of Christ*.[4] Different essays from the fruitful pen of Dr. Warfield are presented again, and it is evidently the supposition of the editor that these studies are a useful contribution to our time, even though Dr. Warfield died in 1921.

It is interesting to compare the spirit of Dr. Nixon's book with that of Dr. Warfield. Dr. Nixon would take a broad view of the importance of the Council of Chalcedon, but Dr. Warfield was stoutly attached to its precise doctrine which he wished to justify by a sober scriptural philology. Dr. Nixon's work is not "polemical" even though he is opposing

---

[4] Benjamin Breckinridge Warfield, *The Person and Work of Christ* edited by Samuel C. Craig (Philadelphia: The Presbyterian and Reformed Publishing Company, 1950).

a whole school of thought, while Dr. Warfield was consciously and earnestly jousting with men of his time. The gravity of a knight in armor and the formality of a tournament fought in high seriousness according to an etiquette characterize the Warfield studies. One meets again the names of Renan, Jülicher, Zahn, Hahn, Swete, and the Schweitzer of the "historical Jesus" days. The heavy philological apparatus, the lengthy footnote, the aloof objectivity, so dear to the last years of the nineteenth and the first fifteen of the twentieth century stir up memories of times gone by. There is much solid scholarship in these essays along with a forthright attack on the liberal theology in full flower during the writer's life. However, it makes strange reading today, and we can appreciate why Dr. Nixon wishes to get away from this type of theology. It has so little to say to our people, and it is difficult to know if this be a criticism of our age or of the stodgy theology of the historicists.

But the kind of work done by Protestant theologians of the first quarter of this century can be continued in a fashion more in accord with the prejudices of the midcentury. This is made patent in the work of Rudolf Bultmann, *Theologie des Neuen Testaments.*[5] Superficially this seems to be a theological investigation very like those made by Dr. Warfield, but even a casual perusal shows that it is a philology quite different from that in vogue in the early years of the twentieth century. The footnotes are few nor are they long. The analysis of the New Testament documents is made not in terms of lexicographical research but by interpreting key words of the text in the light of a unifying theory produced by an existentialist intuition of the meaning of the whole. A theology is being presented and not merely a philological

[5] Rudolf Bultmann, *Theologie des Neuen Testaments, Erste Lieferung* (Tübingen: J. C. B. Mohr [Paul Siebeck], 1948).

commentary or a critical atomism. Harnack, Pfleiderer, Gunkel, and the old trusties of yesterday are not quoted. Schweitzer and Bousset are mentioned and used but they are really transitional figures. Even Catholic scholars are given a special place in the introductory bibliography. It is clearly a different treatment than we were given forty years ago.

It is also different in its content. There is no "quest of the historical Jesus," and instead we have a theology given in terms of the teaching of the original Jesus, its modification and expansion by the evolving Church, and the personal synthesis of Paul. Many of the questions that years ago were treated with pages and chapters are now dismissed with a sentence.[6] Christ's message is no longer the brotherhood of man under the fatherhood of God, an idea so dear to the old liberals, but rather a cry of protest as Barth would like it, and a preaching of God as the source of demand on men whom He meets in a personal encounter.[7] The notion of the Church is now recognized as a true Biblical idea, evolved by a growing Christian community which was always conscious of itself as an eschatological *Qāhāl.*[8] In Paul this Church becomes the Body of Christ, the eschatological congregation of the elect, whose initiation formula is baptism and whose bond of union is the Eucharistic Supper, though neither one nor the other works its effects except as the dramatic Christian preaching of the Christian hope.[9]

All this is so different from the work of the old critical theologians and the only thing left of their thought is the acceptance of the Schweitzerian eschatological Christ; but even here we note a change. Not only is the Kingdom

---

[6] E.g., on p. 27 a single short affirmation tells us with extreme brevity that Messias and Son of Man are two names for the eschatological saviour, without any difference in meaning.

[7] *Op. cit.,* pp. 10–25.

[8] *Op. cit.,* pp. 38 ff.

[9] *Op. cit.,* pp. 302 ff.

preached as coming but as already present in its dawn. Its full morning splendor is left to the future, for the early Christian hope as manifested in the New Testament is a new world to come, according to the teaching of Jesus, now accepted as the Christ.[10]

It is interesting to note the simultaneous appearance of Warfield's and Bultmann's works. It means the tacit by-passing of liberal criticism in modern Protestant thought. The work of the liberal days which is republished is the effort of an adversary of the dominant figures of that period, and the modern continuation of their efforts is executed in a way quite alien to their mode of procedure. There is as much of Barth in Bultmann as there is of Ritschl and Harnack; in fact there is more. Of the great men of 1910 only Schweitzer has survived vitally, and he in their time told the historicists that they were trying to gather figs from thistles. However, the spirit of Harnack is not dead altogether. Evidently accepting certain conclusions of the older critics as definitive, Bultmann tells us that the present Synoptic Gospels are stories that rest on *Urmarkus,* a book whose existence is postulated, and on Q, the catalogue of Jesus-sayings dimly visaged in positive research. These elements were put together along with legendary and anecdotal traditions by a growing Church anxious to justify its own institutions. The complete work passed through the hands of various editors who gave literary unity to the whole, until a universally accepted version became the common property of Christianity.[11] This much, at least, sounds like the Protestant theology of fifty years ago.

However, neither Warfield nor Bultmann represents the most typical theological thinking of modern Protestantism. The most brilliant work is done in what Protestants call

[10] Cf. *op. cit.,* pp. 6–9, 38 ff.
[11] *Op. cit.,* p. 2.

dogmatics. This is not exactly what in Catholic circles is labeled as dogmatic theology, but it is very similar, though it can be projected into a wider framework to become what Dr. Paul Tillich names philosophical theology. The sheerly philological approach is not congenial to the modern mind, and Professor Tillich considers such an attack helpful and legitimate, but not to the point.[12] The best known contributors in the dogmatic field, though not necessarily the ablest contributions, are Karl Barth and Emil Brunner. They are hardly new names but some of their newer works are on the bookstore shelves.

Dogmatics in Outline is the English title for the lectures given by Karl Barth in the Bonn summer school of 1946.[13] The small book is a Barthian theology explained by pegging it onto the Apostles' Creed. According to Barth's own preface, he had to lecture without manuscript under the adverse conditions of the postwar situation. The lectures were taken down as he gave them and these were slightly polished by the author. He warns us that there is nothing in these lectures that will not be found at greater length in his *magnum opus, Kirchliche Dogmatik.* Now Barth's work is frankly and exclusively dogmatic. It is overtly and consciously systematic. There is a full theology outlined in this little book, and what is more important, there is a discussion of the meaning of theology.

Barth's concept of this discipline cannot but interest a modern theologian. Without it, his doctrine in detail can well be misunderstood. A theologian like Warfield would be pleased to read Barth's doctrine concerning God and Jesus Christ, but he would be misled if he believed that he and Barth were in agreement. Concerning Jesus, Barth seems to teach the

[12] Cf. my article, "Contemporaneous Protestantism and Paul Tillich," *Theological Studies,* XI (1950), 177–202.

[13] Karl Barth, *Dogmatics in Outline* translated by G. T. Thomson (New York: Philosophical Library, 1949).

same doctrine that is proposed by the Nicene Synod and he quotes it approvingly.[14] According to Barth, Jesus Christ is true God, true Son of God, God made man. This seems to be an unreserved profession of faith in the divinity of Jesus Christ, but I doubt if Barth means by the terms what Warfield and Thomas Aquinas understood by them. To Warfield's possible question: Is Jesus really what the words, Son of God, true God, mean? Barth would give an evasive answer. He would simply consider any abstract notion of divinity as irrelevant to the discussion. Any philosophic content in the words is not affirmed by Barth, because he believes that such abstractions should not be attributed to the God whom he has met in faith through Jesus the Christ.

I said that God is He who, according to Holy Scripture, exists, lives and acts and makes Himself known. By this definition something fundamentally different is taking place from what would happen, if I should try and set before you conceptually arranged ideas of an infinite, supreme Being. In such a case I would be speculating. But I am not inviting you to speculate. I maintain that this is a radically wrong road which can never lead to God, but to a reality called so only in a false sense. God is He who is to be found in the book of the Old and New Testament, which speaks of Him. And the Christian definition of God consists simply in the statement, "He is spoken of there, so let us listen to what is said of Him there." [15]

And it is part of this, that God is not only unprovable and unsearchable, but also *inconceivable*. No attempt is made in the Bible to define God—that is, to grasp God in our concepts. In the Bible God's name is named, not as philosophers do it, as the name of a timeless Being, surpassing the world, alien and supreme, but as the name of the living, acting, working Subject who makes Himself known.[16]

[14] *Op. cit.*, pp. 85–87.
[15] *Op. cit.*, p. 37.
[16] *Op. cit.*, p. 38.

Now this doctrine indicates an epistemology of purest existentialism, although Barth does not wish to be committed to this philosophy. That which is known in Barthian faith is something that we cannot express conceptually, even when we use concepts to do so, for just how are we to express ourselves except by concepts? Consequently the Barthian acceptation of the Nicene formula for Jesus Christ, or of the term *filioque* in the explanation of the procession of the Spirit,[17] does not commit Barth to any philosophic explanation of these dogmas.

What does he understand by the formulas? He does understand something.

The Creed of Christian faith rests upon knowledge. And where the Creed is uttered and confessed knowledge should be, is meant to be, created. Christian faith is not irrational, not anti-rational, not supra-rational, but rational in the proper sense. The Church which utters the Creed, which comes forward with the tremendous claim to preach and to proclaim the glad tidings, derives from the fact that it has apprehended something—*Vernunft* comes from *vernehmen*—and it wishes to let what it has apprehended be apprehended again. . . . *Pistis* rightly understood is *gnosis;* rightly understood the act of faith is also an act of knowledge. Faith means knowledge.[18]

Here we are faced with something hard to understand. We truly know God. By faith we have a rational grasp of the Creator, yet we are told that we do not know Him by concepts, for He is inconceivable. What kind of knowledge is this? [19] This question is never answered with satisfactory clarity. We are told that faith-knowledge is the old scriptural *sophia,* knowledge that looks to life and action.[20] It is not a thing for itself,

---

[17] *Op. cit.,* p. 44.

[18] *Op. cit.,* pp. 22–23.

[19] It must be noted that for Barth faith is not merely knowledge; it is primarily trust; cf. *op. cit.,* pp. 15–21.

[20] *Op. cit.,* p. 25.

but something that is wholly oriented to a total human activity. It is not the presentation of a picture that may be studied, but rather a beginning of action, which has become luminous by faith-knowledge and which is the flower of that knowledge. However, faith-knowledge is no help to speculation nor a stimulus to it.

If it is safe to interpret this doctrine, I might venture to say that faith gives me knowledge similar to that received when I am put into the vicinity of a fire. I experience its warmth; I see the glow; I am delighted with the play of colors and form: I know fire—but my knowledge includes no theory. Besides, no conception could give me this knowledge, for no conception can produce in me the experienced reality of fire. You may explain fire by the Aristotelian element-theory, by the Phlogiston-theory, by the modern incandescent-change-of-state-theory, but none of these theories will give you, or enter into, the reality of the heat, colors, form, and glow of fire. I cannot prove that I saw fire, and I need no proof for it, because it has impressed itself on me imperiously. The way I conceive it and describe it conceptually is indifferent. The most I can do with such language is to stimulate the listener to experience what I have experienced.

In theology, then, according to Barth we begin after having achieved a meeting with God. This meeting took place through meeting Christ in the Scriptures. Hence it can be said that in the Bible we meet God because we meet His Christ. This happens through no efficacy of our own but because God freely comes to our encounter. From this meeting of person with person, the foundation of theology, the knowledge of God, is given. All theological formulas, therefore, are only testimonies to the initial encounter. They do not explain what we have met; they are explained by what we have met. This does not mean that all formulas are equally valid. Some deny the content of the knowledge from encounter, and these must be rejected. So the Church did when she fought bitterly about an iota in the days of Arianism. The iota denied that Christ was God, and the whole truth of the Scripture is that in Christ we meet God, and therefore He is God.

Consequently Barth with patient condescension admits that the philosophy of the Nicene Fathers was innocent folly and even alien to the revelation, but it supplied a verbal form, fitted to the Greek mind, which could carry the truth of revelation, namely, that Christ is God.[21] Through the Nicene formula the Church confessed what she knew by faith-knowledge achieved through her encounter with Christ and God in the Bible.

This particular mode of theologizing has the advantage of leaping over all the obstacles that harass the theologians who use a different approach. However, it is no longer a rational theology, even though Barth says that faith is rational in its proper sense. By his notion of faith, a *Kennen* is possible but not a *Wissen*. But theology should be a *Wissenschaft* and not merely an ineffable *Erkenntniss*. This verbal distinction is possible in most European languages where there are two words for knowing: *cognoscere* and *scire*. Not every knowledge is *scientia,* because such knowing says something more than mere *cognitio*.

It is quite interesting to see how Barth wishes to eliminate philosophy and speculation from his existentialist theology, but a reflection will tell any thinker that existentialism is a theory and a philosophy. Would anyone wish to go so far as to say that Scripture and the act of faith teach this philosophy? And if they do, how can we accept as valid the general proposition that faith prescinds from philosophic speculation? And if such precision is granted, how can we do justice to the *logos* in theology? An orderly witness to revelation is possible, a witness expressed in language that will be an effica-

<hr/>

[21] *Op. cit.,* pp. 85–86.

cious pointing of the finger to the reality encountered in Scripture, but not a rational scheme which relies on the validity of concepts as the dynamism of its procedure.

To read Karl Barth is like reading a twentieth century reincarnation of Luther. I think that Karl Barth would be pleased with such an evaluation of his message. Moreover, such an affirmation is not the offspring of mere whimsy, for Barth has the passion of Luther, his impetuosity, his forthrightness, his Olympian disdain for critical objections, his high enthusiasm for Scripture. Even the Lutheran attitude to Catholicism is reproduced. Luther had no quarrel with Catholicism as he conceived it, and he believed himself to be a true Catholic. He merely objected, more violently than Barth, to the scheme of Christianity proposed by the official champions of the Roman Church. He could object and protest on the basis of his encounter with Christ in the Scriptures. However, Luther was not a conscious existentialist, though an existentialist drive is transparent in his work. He still tried to use reason and concepts in his polemics against his adversaries.

This very likeness to Luther makes us fear that Karl Barth's thought will have the same fate that his predecessor's had. Men are not satisfied with a mere encounter with Christ, because no encounter is meaningful until it is made intelligible by a concept. Luther and Barth are unconcerned with concepts, but their unconcern is not shared by others who are attracted by their message. The next step in the evolution of Barthianism will be the second step of the evolution of Lutheranism. The concept will come up for discussion and then two distinct lines of development will come to light. One line will reject the concept as a legitimate instrument for the understanding of faith, and we shall have an arational sentimentalism as the soul of religion after the fashion of the theology of Schleiermacher. Simultaneously the other line will analyze the possible meaning of concept. If the philosophy of this second group is positivism, which is nothing but a refinement of the nominalism of the Middle Ages, the truth of faith will be watered down to become a naturalistic consideration of values. If the philosophy to be adopted is the realism of the Thomist vision, the Catholic acceptation of revelation will be inevitable. In other words, the Barthian position is only possible for a short time. It cannot be a stable foundation for belief or theology.

Moreover it is vulnerable to a more urgent attack. It is inspiring to say that we encounter God and His Christ in Scripture. It is a scintillating phrase. However, it is clearly a metaphor. I know what it means to meet John Jones on the street. But certainly I do not meet God in that way in the Bible or in any other historical framework. The mystic seems to encounter God; he experiences Him as an empirical "thou," but mysticism is not natural knowledge. What Barth and the other Neo-Orthodox theologians mean by meeting God in the Scripture is that they had an experience, singular and exhilarating, while reading or pondering the scriptural affirmations. They then attach the experience to a reality, but neither they nor anyone else knows whether the attachment is valid or not. We do not know, nor do they, whether or not they have merely rationalized their experience or whether they have personified a stimulus whose true nature they do not understand. The Scripture tells us that no man has seen God and lived. Far be it from me to attempt a precise interpretation of these words, but the phrase can certainly be used to express the common persuasion that man acting according to his natural processes of knowledge does not experience God. This common persuasion makes a man look with perplexity on the Barthian insistence that we experienced the Lord, for meeting Him can only mean experiencing Him. Until Barth and his colleagues can explain just what this "meeting" is, they will not be able to move men. It is not fair to harp on "meeting" God, because Barth cannot wish to say that we meet God as we meet John Jones, and therefore he is using the word "meeting" in a different sense. One cannot help but desire an explanation of this basic word.

Nor is it very satisfactory to answer that unless one has had the experience one cannot know what it is. This answer is either a banal truism or an evasion. Every experience, simply because it belongs to a closed, unique subject, is ineffable, but that does not mean that it cannot be validly expressed conceptually. My experience of red is incommunicable, but redness can be defined objectively, and not just described with pointings. It is here that we find the root philosophic dogma latent in Barthian thought: concepts are not grasps of reality but the mere human contrivances of relating experiences to each other. We are back to epistemology again and we are faced with an epistemological doctrine which Christianity until the Reformation had successfully rejected. For the Church concepts were important not because they were apt means whereby a witness to an experienced revelation could be made, but because concepts expressed adequately, even though not comprehensively, the revelation received. For the Church revelation is not only a passing experience but also an abiding truth which has an adequate conceptual expression. Barth uses the word truth and declares revelation to be a communication of truth—but he is hemmed in by the traditional Protestant inability to define it.

In the light of these observations on the Barthian work it need hardly be said that a Catholic gains no great satisfaction on reading Barth's seemingly orthodox explanation of the articles of the Apostles' Creed. He believes in God, the God of the Bible. He believes that God is one in three persons, though he tells us that this only means that God exists and acts in three ways.[22] Is this fourth-century modalism come back to life? Barth insists energetically on the divinity of Jesus Christ, according to the Nicene Creed. He believes in the reality and divinity of the Holy Spirit. Yet all these affirmations—and their sincerity cannot be doubted in the slightest—have as much value as the meanings attached to the words. But such meanings will be expressed by concepts, and toward concepts Barth is rather cavalier. In one place, speaking of God's reconciling mankind, he says: "Do not confuse my theory of the reconciliation with the thing itself. All theories of reconciliation can be but pointers." [23] In another place he says

. . . We must remember that everything will depend upon the Christians not painting for the non-Christians in word and deed a *picture* of the Lord or an *idea* of Christ, but on their succeeding with their human words and ideas in pointing to Christ Himself. For it is not the conception of Him, not the dogma of Christ that is the real Lord, but He who is attested in the word of the Apostles.[24]

All these expressions tell me that I simply do not know what Barth means when he speaks of God and His Christ. I personally believe that I have "met" Christ, but I sincerely do not know whether Barth and I have met the same Christ.

However, if our enthusiasm is not engendered by Barthian orthodoxy, yet it is brought forth by his warmth and rich appreciation of obscurer facets of Christian doctrine. He expounds the meaning of Christ's mediation [25] in so forceful and satisfactory a fashion that it is no exaggeration to say that the Franciscan theology which he follows in the matter

[22] *Op. cit.,* p. 42.
[23] *Op. cit.,* p. 116.
[24] *Op. cit.,* p. 94.
[25] *Op. cit.,* pp. 88–94.

has never been presented with greater clarity or greater vigor. This is also true for so many of the Christian dogmas which his brilliance presents with singular charm.

In line with this kind of theology is Emil Brunner's *The Christian Doctrine of God.*[26] This volume is the first of his complete dogmatic theology. It treats of the notion of theology and the matter Catholics discuss in the treatises *De Deo uno, De Deo trino,* and *De Deo creante.* Again we are struck by the apparent orthodoxy of the doctrine and by the existentialist dynamism of the method.

Yet between Barth and Brunner there are clear differences. Barth is vigorous, impatient, a preacher as much as a theologian. Brunner is tranquil, essentially tolerant, and anxious to see the good in every position and assertion. Brunner's work, like that of Barth, is formally dogmatic and is the beginning of his systematic synthesis. He follows the order of the Apostles' Creed in dividing the matter. However, there is a preoccupation with the concept of theology, and of the 353 pages of the book which deals with three important sections of dogmatic theology, 113 are devoted to the question of what theology is and how it should be constructed.

Brunner agrees with Barth in the following positions: (1) Theology is critical thought's witness to revelation. (2) Revelation is achieved in a personal encounter with Christ. (3) Christ is met in Scripture. (4) Theology is not the affair of a mere individual, but rather the witness of the Church to the revelation she has achieved in her encounter with Christ. (5) Natural theology is impossible, because God can only be known by God's revealing free act. (6) The philosophic elements in dogmatic theology are only human media for the expression and communication of a free divine ex-

[26] Emil Brunner, *The Christian Doctrine of God, Dogmatics,* I, translated by Olive Wyon (Philadelphia: The Westminster Press, 1950).

perience. They are pointers to the truth but not adequate expressions of it.

In other words, Brunner and Barth are in basic agreement concerning the nature of the theological task. The differences will be found within the same framework of thought. For example, Brunner leans more to Calvin than he does to Luther. Again, his treatment of the trinitarian problem is more consistent with his basic postulates. In consequence, according to Brunner, the question of three in one must not be explained at all. We meet this truth in revelation, but we meet no metaphysical principle or explanation there. Hence just how it is, we do not know, nor does its truth shed light on an abstract problem. In this way Barthian modalism is not needed. It is simply true that God is the Father, God is the Son, God is the Holy Ghost, and this truth is found in the Scripture. Outside of that context we know absolutely nothing about it or about any related problem. In revelation there is no metaphysics entailed or given. To put it simply, we know that God is triune, but we do not know what that means, though we know that it is true. Any philosophy of person, substance, and triplicity is excluded from the revelation, and if the Church did use such philosophic explanation, it was without commitment to it and as a mere pointer to the truth met in faith. Where an attempt is made to include such metaphysical speculation in the content of the formulas of revelation, the theologian must resist and protest. The theologian is a witness to faith and not a scientist.

As a mode of Christian doctrine, as a function of the Church itself, dogmatics has primarily no interest in being called a "science." Its primary tendency is certainly not in the direction of intellectual research, but in the direction of the fellowship of faith and the preaching of the Church. The earliest theology of the Church betrays no "academic" aspirations of any kind. It is, therefore, really an open question whether dogmatics can have an interest in being called a "science" and in having to satisfy any kind of intellectual criteria.[27]

For all these reasons the "scientific" character of dogmatics, if we want to use this terminology at all, is *sui generis;* it can be compared with no other "science"; it must be measured by its own criteria, and it operates with its own methods, peculiar to itself, and unknown in any other science.[28]

It will be quite clear from these words that the theologian must follow the teaching of the Church, but, unlike the Catholic theologian who does so because the Church gives him the revelation adequately expressed in intelligible dogmas, the Brunner theologian finds the meaning of the dogma not by philosophical or philological research, but in the experience of the revelation in its source, the Bible. The Brunner theologian criticizes the Church's dogma by an experience stimulated by the Bible. He understands the dogma by the Bible but never the Bible by the dogma. It is true that he never "understands" the Bible at all, if by understanding we mean a conceptual grasp of the thing, although there is a different kind of understanding, namely, the knowledge of experience.

In consequence, when dealing with God, Brunner does not consider Him under the headings of the divine attributes usually proposed in Catholic and Protestant dogmatic treatises as orientations for the study of God. The reason for this procedure is that such an orientation would be the introduction of a metaphysic as the framework for an understanding of the divine. This, in Brunner's thought, is impossible. Instead he considers God not according to attributes derived *a priori,* but rather according to the properties that Scripture gives to God: God as Lord, God as holy, God as love. Brunner will not admit any reasoning that derives from divine at-

[27] *Op. cit.,* p. 60.
[28] *Op. cit.,* p. 63.

tributes predicated of God as necessarily flowing from His essence. What is more, Brunner dislikes the word necessity as an epithet for God, for God is free and in freedom He is related to the world and in freedom He is known. In like manner man's approach to God is also in freedom, and therefore this Calvinist theologian rejects the whole Calvinist doctrine of predestination as unscriptural. Instead of Calvinism, Brunner teaches that the only doctrine of the Bible on this subject is that man cannot know God except God reveal Himself to him. God's revelation is grace, gratuitous and not necessary. From that point on, however, there is no determination of man, who freely accepts the revelation and freely brings it to term. According to Brunner, Calvin and the other Reformers saw this truth but they did not express it properly because they brought in metaphysical notions by which they tried to understand it. The introduction of metaphysics as content of revelation is always illegitimate. It has a function, but it is a humble one, which consists in indicating a truth to be grasped without metaphysics.

Brunner here betrays the weakness of the Neo-Orthodoxy. It is equally evident in Barth. Whether these theologians admit it or not, they teach the double truth that Thomas Aquinas worked so hard to eliminate from theology. Throughout Neo-Orthodoxy runs tacitly this basic proposition: God is unknowable to man's intellect as a faculty of conceptualization. The Neo-Orthodox theology attempts to overcome this primary impossibility by making the knowledge of God possible outside the structure of conceptualization through the medium of personal encounter, which is conditioned by God who can reveal Himself if He freely wishes it. This is the anti-intellectualism of the Reformation, and it has remained in Protestantism unto our day. Existentialism is a philosophy that is most congenial to this position, and it is no wonder that it was conceived by a fervent Protestant and enthusiastically accepted by many

Protestant thinkers as the philosophic background without which no theology can be constructed. To the Neo-Orthodox position St. Thomas would insist that knowing is an action of the human intellect, one and unique. It knows not by mere encounter but by illuminating the encounter with concepts. There can be no knowledge on the connatural human plane where concepts are eliminated and there can be no concepts without a metaphysic implied. The perennial Protestant urge to get rid of metaphysics is a futile rebellion. You cannot eliminate metaphysics from connatural human knowledge and every attempt to do so must perforce be metaphysical. If God is not grasped in terms of metaphysics, He is not grasped meaningfully at all. It is true that pure a priori reasoning cannot discover God,—and that is why Aquinas rejected the ontological argument as a valid approach to Him. God must be met in existence, and only there can we find Him, but it is an existence illuminated by metaphysics. Without it existence and its resulting experiences are meaningless.

Existentialism necessarily makes much of freedom. Now freedom is a fact in human life and it is a basic fact in God's relation to this world. However, freedom must not be so stressed that necessity disappears from the picture. Freedom supposes necessity, without which it is meaningless, for it can only be defined in terms of the necessary. Before existence can say freedom, it must suppose necessity. The first Existent has rightly been considered in Christian thought as the necessary Being. To reject all this on the ground that it is a "metaphysic," is the rejection of thought itself, for thought is a metaphysical commitment. This is an existential fact, and an appeal to existence does not escape it but rather discovers it luminously.

It is clear, therefore, that Brunner's existentialism raises many objections that make us uneasy with his theology. However, it gives to theology certain values that make this science most precious. If anti-intellectualism is a suicidal plunge into nothingness, so too pure rationalism is a fatal curtailment of reality. Faith is not a rationalism, nor is theology, which is the science of faith. Theology is eminently reasonable, and it has no quarrel with reason which it necessarily but gladly uses as an instrument. However, theology should have a warmth which is more than the glow of satisfaction which meets the abstract thinker when he glimpses a vast structure of truth. At the end of his consideration of the nature and role of theology, Brunner beautifully describes this added thing that theology should give.

[Dogmatics] is not the mistress, but the servant of faith and of the community of believers; and its service is no less, but also no more, than the service of *thought* to faith. Its high dignity consists in the fact that it is a service to the highest final truth, to that truth which is the same as true love, and it is this which gives it the highest place in the realm of thought. But the fact that it is no more than this service of *thought*—which, as such, does not maintain that love and loyalty which must be expected from the Christian—is its limitation; a dogmatic which is aware of this, shows it is genuine. The dogmatic theologian who does not find that his work drives him to pray frequently and urgently, from his heart: "God, be merciful to me a sinner," is scarcely fit for his job.[29]

A pure existentialist theology is not the only theological form being evolved in modern Protestantism. One of the most significant events in the 1949 meeting of the American Theological Society (Protestant) was the presidential address of Dr. W. Norman Pittenger of the General Theological Seminary of New York. He called his contribution "The Theological Enterprise and the Life of the Church." [30]

[29] *Op. cit.*, p. 85.
[30] W. Norman Pittenger, "The Theological Enterprise and the Life of the Church," *Anglican Theological Review*, XXXI (1949), 189–196.

The matrix of Dr. Pittenger's conception of theology is identical with that of the Catholic vision, though he has elements in his theory which Catholic theologians would exclude. Of course, Dr. Pittenger, an Anglo-Catholic, would promptly point out that he never wished to do anything else but give a Catholic theory of theology, but I am sure that he will at least smilingly bear with me if I use the word "Catholic" as identical with the term, Roman Catholic, and "Protestant" as applicable to all western forms of Christian belief other than Roman Catholicism.

What is noteworthy in Dr. Pittenger's address is that he stressed in a Protestant theological atmosphere the following points:

1) Theology, and precisely dogmatic theology, is important and its importance is clearly felt by Protestants today.

2) The theologian does not simply pick and choose among Christian doctrines in order to erect a theory to his own liking, but he must give an intellectual synthesis of the whole Christian tradition as expressed in Scripture and in the continuous life and teaching of the Church from her beginnings to our time.

3) The theologian is an intellectual worker and he proceeds intellectually on the data of revelation as given in Scripture and tradition. He cannot consider revelation outside its intellectual setting, and therefore the principles of thought valid in all thought disciplines are equally valid in theology. There are not two kinds of truth: truth in revelation and truth outside of revelation; the order of truth is one.

4) However, rationalism, that is, the restriction of knowledge to the field of naturally achievable truth, cannot be the framework of theology, because the data of revelation go beyond the restrictions of pure reason, although not against its norms. Reason is employed by the theologian as a tool, but it is only one tool, nor is it ever the implement of dis-

covery. Intellectualism must not be identified with rationalism.

5) A valid natural theology is not only conceivable but necessary as the prelude and apologetic for theology.

6) Theology must be a Christian enterprise. It must not stay exclusively on the plane of theory but it must become and be a more intense and total incorporation of the theologian into the total life of the Mystical Body of Christ, which is His Church.

These propositions are certainly the backbone of that theological method which produced Origen, Cyprian, Basil and the Cappadocians, Augustine, Anselm, Thomas Aquinas, Bonaventure, Cajetan, Bellarmine, Newman, Scheeben, and the other universally recognized representatives of a genuine Christian theology. Dr. Pittenger has clearly indicated the way of avoiding the Scylla and Charybdis of naturalistic rationalism and extreme existentialism. His insistence that theology should be an incentive to Christian piety corresponds beautifully to the frequent demands for the vitalization of theological theory which are found in modern Catholic literature and which were met partially in the *corollaria et scholia practica* that gave a special winsomeness to Father Hugo Hurter's theological manuals. It is no wonder that a Catholic theologian cannot help but find deep satisfaction in Dr. Pittenger's outline of theological method.

However, would the Protestant reaction be the same? As this article shows, liberalism, historicism, and existentialism are dynamisms which are at work in the contributions of the best known modern Protestant theologians. Would not the Protestant spirit of enquiry scorn Dr. Pittenger's blueprint of a valid divinity? The late Dr. Edgar Brightman would certainly answer in the affirmative.

. . . The experiences recorded in the Bible and in other sacred literatures are regarded as data for investigation just like any other experiences; no authority attaches to them other than the authority of experience and reason. For theologians who take this point of view (including most contemporary American Protestant thinkers in the field such as A. C. Knudsen, W. A. Brown, H. N. Wieman, John Bennett, R. L. Calhoun, W. M. Horton, and others), theology is a branch of philosophy of religion. It differs from philosophy of religion simply in the nature of its starting point. . . . For theology, the historical beliefs of the theologian's own religious community are the primary sources. Theology thus has a more restricted field as its starting point; but the materials of this field are studied by the same critical and rational methods as philosophy applies in any field. If the theologian maintains his ideal thus set up, he is a philosopher of religion engaged in a peculiarly thorough and critical philosophical interpretation of the subject matter of some one religious faith. Unfortunately, it sometimes happens that preoccupation with one tradition tends to produce a bias in favor of that tradition which renders objectivity all but impossible.[31]

Brightman himself followed this method in his theological work, and according to the words quoted, so do the majority of American Protestant theologians. Dr. Pittenger is not unaware of these facts, but he probably felt that many Protestant theologians were dissatisfied with this approach to the problem. He does make an overt observation concerning this kind of theology.

It does not seem possible, in my opinion, to call by the adjective "Christian" an enterprise such as that which I once found described in a summer-session announcement: "The Christian Faith. After lectures by the instructor, the student will construct his own statement of belief, on the basis of his study of the New Testament, modern philosophy, and the scientific world-view." That curious description would seem more appropriate to some bright new variety of "christianized theism" than to the attempt to appropriate the Christian faith in all of its historic richness, finding in it a reason for living and a meaning for life.[32]

[31] Edgar Sheffield Brightman, *A Philosophy of Religion* (New York: Prentice-Hall, 1949), p. 24.
[32] W. Norman Pittenger, *op. cit.*, p. 191.

It may well be that Dr. Pittenger's reaction to this kind of theology was shared by others at the theological meeting, but I fear that very many considered ideal that which Dr. Pittenger found so strange.

Even for those who felt that Dr. Pittenger was right, a formidable problem was raised. There seems to be a widespread feeling among Protestant theologians, at least in this country, that theology must deal with the teaching of the Church and not only with the doctrines of the Bible. In fact, it is today quite clear that the theory of Article VIII of the Thirty-nine Articles will not meet reality. We cannot understand Christian dogma by the Bible, but rather we must understand the Bible by the dogma. For the Protestant this becomes a heartrending task, for he must decide what is valid dogma and what is not. The Catholic can always turn to a fixed living norm, the authoritative magisterium, but the Protestant will not recognize this test, nor has he anything objective and definitive to put in its place. He must rest content with his own personal opinion sincerely achieved after much study of the history of the Church, stifling all doubts with the hope that he was guided by the Holy Spirit. This is not unlike the action of the summer-session student who constructed his own statement of belief.

In spite of the strong voices that are today heard in Protestant theological circles in favor of a divine science according to the ancient Christian tradition, the Protestant cannot overcome the impulse toward church building. It will always be so because the principle of protest cannot admit that the Mystical Body of Christ, the Church, exists with an indestructible structure and an infallible teaching power whose pronouncements are enlightenment for the mind and not objects of criticism. This Protestant situation derives from Protestant theology's inability to answer Pilate's question: "What is truth?"

8

✢✢✢

Protestantism as a
Catholic Concern

✢✢✢

IN THE days of the First World War I was a grammar-school boy. The neighborhood manifested our characteristic American religious pluralism. Our preadolescent group was made up of Catholics and Protestants, roughly half and half. We went to different schools but after school hours we were together. My closest friend, to whom I was closely attached, was a Lutheran boy.

As a group we rarely talked about religion or church. It is hard today to explain this reticence, but I suspect that boys do not discuss religion much, and besides we were unconsciously shrewd enough not to raise questions which would divide us; for our union was strong and happy. Yet I remember talking once about religion with my Lutheran friend, and he mentioned that in his church the minister wore vestments like our Catholic priests. I doubt if the vestments in that day were more than a Geneva gown and surplice. However, my friend pointed to a fact which was basic in our religious lives. There was a fundamental similarity in the two religions. He and I were both taught the Apostles' Creed, whose articles with the exception of the one on the Catholic Church we understood in much the same way. We were both taught by our respective churches that there was a transcendent God. We believed in the divinity of Jesus of Nazareth, Christ, our Lord. We believed in His Virgin Birth. We believed that Easter Sunday was the memorial of His rising from the tomb in the flesh, after His saving death for us. We were taught that there was a Holy Spirit, and the Father, Son, and Spirit were three distinct persons in one Godhead. We were prepared to look for the final judgment when we should rise bodily from the dead to enter into life everlasting.

Our morality was substantially the same. We were not supposed to lie; we had to respect our elders; it was wrong to steal or destroy other people's property; we were not to do "dirty things," concerning which our notions were disturbingly vague and hidden in silence. It was a matter of course that we should go to church on Sunday in our best clothes, which more than the holiness of the day prevented us from practicing the sports and games of weekdays. There was at that time a conscious and willed Catholic-Protestant division; but actually we were less divided in belief and conduct than today, when such divisions are strongly deprecated.

Since the First World War, Catholic and Protestant theologies have undergone changes. This is hardly noteworthy, because the human discipline of theology like all human disciplines develops and evolves. However, what is noteworthy is that in the Protestant grassroots a change has taken place which is more than theological. It is in belief itself. The 'twenties saw the Protestants break into two very different and hostile camps. Fundamentalism pulled together and closed its ranks against the liberals. It was not sect against sect, but rather traditional belief against a reconstructed faith, and the same battle was fought in all the sects. That war is still going on, but one side is winning. In spite of strong visible fundamentalist militancy, in our metropolitan areas and to a lesser degree even in the rural areas liberalism is giving the tone to national church doctrine.

The Protestant crisis is domestic to Protestantism. Catholics have no right or desire to take part in the quarrel. However, the change of Protestantism produces a change in the environment in which the American Catholic lives. Protestant beliefs have repercussions on the Catholic believer, and Catholics have cause for intranquillity because of what they see about them.

It is paradoxical that the one article of the Creed which once clearly separated Protestant from Catholic, the article concerning the universal or Catholic Church, is no longer so divisive. Thanks to the ecumenical movement, many Protestants are tentatively formulating a concept of the Church which timorously approaches the Catholic notion; but in the rest of the articles we are today worlds apart. In spite of the efforts of the neosupernaturalists who stress the transcendence of God, many Protestants, clerical and lay, theological and nontheological, identify God with something in man. For an ever-increasing number Jesus of Nazareth is not really God. The Holy Ghost is not a person but only a divine name. Jesus died but did not rise from the dead, except in some mysterious symbolic sense. The Virgin Birth is a first-century legend, not true historically though rich in religious significance. Many Protestants hope there is a future life, but they are not committed to it by their faith. Except for the fundamentalists, many contemporary Protestants have no clear meaning in mind when they say, "I believe in the resurrection of the body."

These reflections are the by-product of the study of three books indicative of American Protestant thought in our time.

It is not for Catholics to decide whether the books genuinely depict the Protestant vision. Yet we cannot ignore the fact that these books reflect the religious visions of a rapidly expanding sector of our Protestant neighbors with whom we wish to and must live.

The first book I refer to is not new. It was written by a scholar, temperate and learned, dean of Drew Theological Seminary. The book is filled with a spirit of genuine but unobtrusive piety coupled with knowledge and high intelligence. The author has died since the book was published over ten years ago. I am speaking of Dean Clarence Tucker Craig's (1895–1953) *The Beginning of Christianity*.[1] How far this book expresses Dean Craig's final thought I cannot say, but it does reflect the mind of many moderate Protestant scholars of our time.

What was Craig's conception of Christianity? That question is obviously primary, because he discussed its early history, and any discussion supposes some understanding of the terms involved. For Dean Craig Christianity is a complex. The complex is made up of two elements. One is the gospel which lies below the surface of the written Gospels; the other is the historical incarnation given to the genuine gospel message by the various cultures which received it. Christianity is a continuous movement of one basic thought. Whatever culture or historical moment achieves it as a dynamic guide for life, receives the message according to its own intellectual and social structure. In consequence, each age drops something and adds something of its own to the nucleus, thus transforming for itself the total formulation. Such transformations are quite legitimate and inevitable; for only in this way can the nuclear simplex dynamically survive.

[1] Clarence Tucker Craig, *The Beginning of Christianity* (New York–Nashville: Abingdon-Cokesbury Press, 1943).

What is the dynamic simplex? Craig answers in italics: "Conduct is Christian when in response to God's forgiving grace men seek to solve their human problems according to the principle of love, using the guidance of Jesus, the best ethical experience of the race, and the fullest possible contemporary knowledge of facts." [2] In accord with this definition and with the contents of the book in general we can draw the conclusion that questions concerning the divinity of Christ or His Virgin Birth or His resurrection are quite irrelevant to Christianity in an age when such elements, added in an earlier epoch, can no longer be maintained. These questions do not belong to the gospel as a simplex, but only to the peripherical complex which is ever changing.

Here is a clear answer to the fundamentalists. To their fundamentals Craig opposes his. The fundamentalists suppose the inerrancy of the scriptural propositions taken individually and literally. Craig rejects such a postulate on the basis of "the fullest possible contemporary knowledge of facts."

Dean Craig had a consistent theory wherewith he could admit both Christian continuity and Christian change. However, in order to construct the theory he had to postulate that Christianity is essentially a solution of the human problems of life. It is an ethics, rendered religious by the introduction of God as a factor; but of course the notion of God is not explained. Jesus is an ethical example, who acted out of a motive of *agape* bolstered by a trust in an ultimate righteous principle who (or which) can rectify our mistakes if only they are dynamized by some degree of unselfishness as their radical drive. In such a doctrine we find elements derived from all the modern leaders of Protestant theology —Barth, Bowne, Bultmann, Nygrén, Temple, and Tillich.

Now this vision is naturalistic, though couched in the

[2] *Ibid.,* pp. 334-335.

old consecrated supernaturalistic terms of forgiveness and grace. The supernatural in the classical understanding of that term has been gently washed out. Theology has become an ambiguous humanistic philosophy. Christ, though given a high place, has been lowered. In fact, one wonders how Craig could consistently give Him such a superlatively high place. If Christ is only an ethical example of heroic size, why should we raise Him above the Buddha? Gautama was an admirable moral example. Yet the perennial Christian missionary effort in Buddhist lands can only be explained by the hypothesis that Christians always believed that Jesus was superior to Moses, Gautama, and the angels.

It is at this point that the Catholic painfully feels concern. There is a growing danger that Catholics and Protestants will live in utterly different and alien dimensions. The words we both use have become so hopelessly equivocal that we have become unintelligible to each other. The modern Protestant in his ecumenicist zeal is anxious to talk to us about the Church; but the whole supernatural context which surrounds that word for us is so foreign to his way of thinking that he cannot conceive that we actually believe in it. He only knows that we are not fundamentalists and because of that fact he unwittingly comes to the conclusion that we are naturalists. Nevertheless, the fundamentalist, though far from the Catholic position, is much nearer to us than his liberal confrere who often enough expresses his belief in the very formulas we use. The fundamentalist still believes in the supernatural; the liberal, paleo- or neo-, does not.

This alarming confusion arises because contemporaneous Protestantism is still bedeviled by the false dilemma: either fundamentalism or liberalism. A Catholic thinks that it must be neither fundamentalism nor liberalism. But in the meantime the naturalism basic to liberalism and Neo-Orthodoxy is producing a cultural climate where the Catholic feels himself estranged from the men he lives with. For us this is a harrowing awareness; for we have been at home in the West since A.D. 313. Moreover, we have always been too sanguine in thinking that the rifts of the sixteenth century could somehow be welded; but now we find that a rapidly growing sector of Protestantism is effectively reducing the meeting ground in the Catholic substance which was preserved by the first Reformers. The Protestant must see that we have reason to be concerned, even though the Protestant crisis, absolutely speaking, is for Protestants alone.

Because of Dean Craig's basic conception of Christianity, much of the good to be achieved by the reading of his book loses its charm. His excellent use of the historical-form theory for the exposition of the Synoptic background does not overcome the feeling that he is using it to serve his naturalistic conception of Christianity. Must Biblical criticism be a foe to supernaturalism? By its own theory and structure there is no such necessity. It has its own field and in that field it serves well. Were it not better to restrict it to that field, without allowing it to intrude into theology itself, where it has no important place? After all, Dean Craig's conception of Christianity is a theological achievement, and theology has its own methods of operation.

But if Dean Craig's scholarly approach to Christianity is disturbing for a Catholic in spite of its scholarship, something short of dismay is evoked by the little book of Kenneth A. Holmes, a Protestant pastor in the Buffalo metropolitan area. The opusculum, *Foes of the Spirit*,[3] is not set on the scholarly level of Dean Craig's book. It is for popular consumption, and is probably a revision of a series of pulpit addresses.

It is a kindly book, with malice toward none. Certainly

[3] Kenneth A. Holmes, *Foes of the Spirit: A Critique of Religious Formalism* (New York: Exposition Press, 1952).

no Catholic has a right to complain that Catholicism is harshly handled, for Mr. Holmes treats the Church very handsomely. Protestant scholars might wonder why this book is considered in a theological essay; for its theological content is neither new nor brilliant. Yet the book is significant for two reasons. First, Mr. Holmes proposes simple old-fashioned liberalism with the clarity and simplicity of a primer. The author's position is not clouded by double talk. He is forthright and unequivocal, with the courage to accept the conclusions of the premises he believes in. Second, this is the doctrine given successfully to a Christian community in the name of the Gospel. This message will consequently seep out into larger areas of Protestant life, constituting for many the blueprint to live by.

Foes of the Spirit is another result of the Protestant dilemma, "either fundamentalism or liberalism." Mr. Holmes was a student of the Bob Jones University of Greenville, South Carolina (the school was named for Bob Jones, the dynamic Southern evangelist), at the same time that the contemporary evangelist, Billy Graham, studied there. His Midwestern home environment was a fitting preparation for the teaching of the fundamentalism of his college, which in turn fitted him for the Baptist seminary he later attended. He became a Baptist minister at the conclusion of his seminary training. However, because of his reading while in the seminary his faith in fundamentalism was shaken, and his study and experience in the ministry finally though painfully killed it altogether.[4] With fundamentalism gone, the only alternative was liberalism. "Either—or."

Mr. Holmes is now the pastor of a nondenominational community church. But conversions are never totally transformative. Mr. Holmes brings much of his old evangelistic "witnessing" fervor to his new home. In fact, he wants to

---

[4] *Ibid.*, pp. 39, 60–63, 83.

engender a prophetic zeal in liberalism, and he speaks of a "prophetic liberalism." [5] It is doubtful if any liberal will welcome Mr. Holmes's suggestion. Liberals have a horror of evangelist pyrotechnics. Even Paul Tillich, who sees in the prophetic protest the very soul of Protestantism, will not wholly approve of the fusion of the gospeler's fire with the liberal's ice.

What is the theological content of Holmesian Christianity?

(1) God is the "inner voice" in man. "God is in man, collectively and individually, continuously speaking His message." [6] ". . . God dwells here and now in every human breast, . . . within me there reside untold latent divine powers!" [7] "I must simply unify myself to follow the highest and best within my own nature. If that is humanism, it is also theism; for the best in humanity is divinity." [8] This latent human power pressing for realization is the Divine Spirit.

God must not be conceived according to the old theologies.

. . . The old theologies taught [that] there is an Almighty God, King of the Universe, seated upon a heavenly throne, Who can at will miraculously intervene in the affairs of men and nations to bring about His desired ends. Such a God died, or at least should have died, at the coming of the democratic era and the emergence of great nations governed by the people. The only Deity truly democratic people know is the God within and among them, the Voice that calls and the Finger that points to the highest and the best.[9]

(2) This basic theology is the spirit and doctrine of Jesus. That "this historical person was born of a virgin, fulfilled numerous Old Testament prophecies, died as an atonement

[5] *Ibid.,* pp. 67, 84.
[6] *Ibid.,* pp. 84–85.
[7] *Ibid.,* p. 85.
[8] *Ibid.*
[9] *Ibid.,* p. 19.

for men's sins, arose bodily from the grave, and ascended physically into heaven" is "myth." [10] Jesus Himself "was a rebel and a heretic." [11] His spirit was humanistic and progressive.

(3) Jesus was not divine in the orthodox sense of the word. "Jesus of Nazareth himself is a symbol, not an object of worship. He is the symbol of the divine possibilities resident within every human creature." [12]

(4) The Jesus of Christianity is not so much a historical person as a high ideal. Because of the little we know of the historical Jesus we have attributed to Christ "the spirit of brotherhood and love . . . which we seek to follow, that spirit which we believe strives for realization in every human life and in the social order." [13] The historical Jesus had His defects, for example, He was a nationalist. "It is not in reality the words and works, the teachings and life, of Jesus that we set before ourselves as examples. Those things, great and good as they may have been in many respects, are too vaguely known, wrapped about as they are in the Gospels with supernaturalism and doctrine and mythology." [14]

(5) "The Christian religion is independent of the Bible." [15] This does not mean that the Bible is insignificant. It is helpful for Christian living; it is inspirational, provocative, stimulating. However, it contains much, both in the Old and New Testaments, which is "sub-Christian and even immoral." [16] The doctrine of the fundamentalists, who teach the supernatural inspiration and inerrancy of the Bible, is bibliolatry.

(6) The Church in its ideal aspect is the body of Christ. "That term, if it means anything, suggests that the Church is

[10] *Ibid.*, p. 33.
[11] *Ibid.*
[12] *Ibid.*, p. 46.
[13] *Ibid.*, p. 56.
[14] *Ibid.*
[15] *Ibid.*, p. 16.
[16] *Ibid.*

in America
rally proper

By educa-
wn poten-
cted, and
imulated
man be-
vity pro-
gdom of
society

Man is
orance.
to the
t man
earth,
ntion

nacy
pirit
uch
ind

th
ly
e

r
r

mbodiment in all succeeding
irit which was seen in Jesus of
. The spirit of brotherhood and
n the Church, not the spirit of
n." [17] However, the historical
from this ideal. "Too often the
f the spirit, a foe of progress." [18]
Church is a major debacle on the re-
palling and tragic condition." [19]
tion of the Church? Obviously it is
t patterns of the past. The doctrines of
nd in the Bible, are not normative;
s progressively to be left behind. There
The Church is here to evolve ever up-
lfillment of the purposes of the Spirit of
se purposes are the actualization of the
es of human nature. The guiding ideas for
t are (a) the equalitarian and loving brother-
, regardless of race, color, or condition; (b)
of human values.[20]

dvances and deepens the brotherhood of man,
es humanity happier and more creative, is good.
e only goods to pursue. The moral norms given
ches and society can be followed, but always
he primary guiding ideas. The codes of religion
lative.

hibition, be it deemed ever so sacred—the Decalogue's
ainst stealing or adultery or murder, the nation's ban
nage or treason, or society's disapproval of drunkenness
ling—whatever it be, it must be considered relative.
the breaching of such a rule, either directly or indirectly,
nore good than harm to mankind in some specific instance,

id., p. 54.
id.
bid., p. 71.
Ibid., pp. 83–87. That there are no final truths, cf. p. 14.

as could quite conceivably be the case, it would be mo
to break the law and bless the man.[21]

(8) How is the Church to achieve its mission?
tion. The only reason man does not realize his o
tialities is ignorance. He must therefore be instru
this instruction, achieved by science, should be s
and abetted by the Church in word and symbol. As
comes more and more educated, he will by his acti
duce on earth the Brotherhood of Man and the Kin
God, which will manifest themselves in a one-world
with a one-world government.

The doctrine of original sin is baneful to religion.
not corrupt, even though capable of evil through ign
Man is born in original virtue, because he is made
image and likeness of God. There are no limits to wha
can do; he can create the Kingdom of God here on
nor need he wait for some spectacular divine interve
for its accomplishment.

(9) Faith in immortality does not threaten the prin
of the temporal. We only hope for a survival of the s
after death, but we know nothing about the modes of s
survival. This hope can have no bearing on our life here,
when the future does come, it will take care of itself[??]

Any student of the history of philosophy confronted wi
the vision offered in the above scheme will immediate
recognize it as the liberalism which died with the end of th
First World War. The great Protestant theologians of ou
time have all rejected it with more or less contempt. Walte
Horton, who has carefully and sympathetically watched
movements in Protestant thought, declares this kind of the
ology *passé*.[23] Yet here it is again, offering immanence, rela-

[21] *Ibid.*, p. 66.
[22] *Ibid.*, pp. 17–18.
[23] Cf. Walter M. Horton, "Systematic Theology: Liberalism Chastened by

tivism, humanistic naturalism, ethicism, the panacea of education, as the essence of Christianity. Mr. Holmes chides the Neo-Orthodox because they are only semiliberals. He does not seem to appreciate that they reject fundamentalism no less than he; but they were compelled to reject liberalism as well, because they found it just as unsatisfactory. Mr. Holmes is going to have a formidable task to persuade our age to take up again what it but recently discarded. The "ever upwards and onwards" slogan of the Unitarians sounds hollow to our contemporary youth, and a childlike faith in the utopian potential of education is difficult for all who no longer believe in Santa Claus. Mr. Holmes learned his liberalism in a fundamentalist preserve.

This is a Protestant pastor's formulation of the Protestant conception of the Gospel message. Far be it from us to enter into a polemic or essay a refutation. The only complaint here registered is that Holmes is using the word "Christianity" in a sense utterly alien to the meanings attached to that word in the course of 2000 years. "Our Father, who art in heaven," seems to indicate a God transcendental to man, something more than an inner voice. Without consulting Christian prayers, let Mr. Holmes consult the curse words used in western cultures. Those words will tell him what the accepted meaning of the words God, Christ, and the future life are, without edification, ambiguity, or equivocation. Of course, Mr. Holmes knows that he is not using the Christian words in their ordinary lexicographic definition, and he defends his right to use them differently.[24] His right is admitted; he can use the words any way he wishes. But would

---

Tragedy," in *Protestant Thought in the Twentieth Century*, ed. Arnold S. Nash (New York: Macmillan, 1951), pp. 117–119.

[24] *Foes of the Spirit*, p. 34: "But I protest that there is nothing dishonest in using these terms with meanings different from those accepted by the fundamentalists. . . . Liberals feel that many of the traditional words of Christianity are good and expressive and should be retained in the more intelligible theology forever in the process of development."

it not be more honest and more candid for him to say forth-
rightly that the historical religion of Christianity, based on
the belief in a transcendental, commanding God, is a pitiable
hoax deriving from an immature human tendency to per-
sonify forces which are intrinsic to nature and man? It seems
more foursquare to say flatly that Christianity, a well defined
historical reality, is a harmful delusion which must be liq-
uidated and supplanted by a romantically naturalistic ethical
culture movement, which will incorporate into itself some of
the valuable elements of the older tradition. This is what
men like Mr. Holmes do not state but what they are actually
doing. They undoubtedly have the civic right to do so. But
to call their product Christianity is as honorable as selling a
South Carolina Baptist a bottle of gin by the device of label-
ing it vegetable compound, and justifying the technique by
pointing out that juniper berries are vegetable.

For Catholics this kind of Christianity is so different from
what they understand by the name that they will be totally
confused by the new usage of the term, "Christianity." For
an ever larger group in our pluralistic society Christianity is
a complete contradiction of all that the other group considers essential to the notion. A unifying common word has
suddenly become a meaningless tag usable for any kind of
thought or conduct. Any man who derives humanistic inspiration from some one or other New Testament concept,
be he a Jew, Brahmin, or atheist, can be called a Christian,
according to men like Mr. Holmes. In such a situation
"Christian" says no more than "human being." But the
epithet, "Christian," says more and always has said more.
The Catholic has a right to protest against a usage of the
word which sucks out of it all that is characteristic, and re-
duces a holy symbol to inanity.

Dean Craig and Mr. Holmes can be depressing to a Catholic, but this must be said for their work: it is an acceptance of

the high task of putting down what they conceive to be the ideas of Christianity. Each in his own fashion is interested in thought and reason. They make concepts and notions clear to the public. A Catholic may be nonplussed by their theology, but it is a theology, constructed in accord with definite principles and in obedience to logic. At least an intelligent analysis is possible, and even invited.

The scene changes utterly when we read *The Power of Positive Thinking* by Dr. Norman Vincent Peale,[25] an ordained Methodist minister, though now pastor of the Marble Collegiate Reformed Church in New York. After reading this book the Catholic theologian gasps and goes limp. The opus does not read like a religious message at all. Rather it has all the aspects of modern high-pressure advertising for some patent medicine which cures every ill known to man. Not all Protestant thinkers look with a kindly eye on Dr. Peale's glad tidings, and Professor William Lee Miller has written a cleverly critical consideration of Dr. Peale's effort.[26]

[25] Norman Vincent Peale, *The Power of Positive Thinking* (New York: Prentice-Hall, 1952).

[26] William Lee Miller, "Some Negative Thinking about Norman Vincent Peale," *Reporter* 12 (January, 1955), 19–24. Concerning Peale's radio and television shows, Dean Liston Pope, of the Yale Divinity School, made some scathing remarks at the annual meeting of the Broadcasting and Film Commission of the National Council of Churches on March 1, 1955: "I would not have believed that anything could be stickier than some of the soap operas, but religion has outdone even Lever Brothers." The brotherhood theme is offered as a "nostrum to keep America strong, in the name of religion." "This kind of thing represents a prostitution of the Christian faith and a crucifixion anew of the Christ who put human brotherhood in the most terrible and demanding of all relationships, that of common Sonship under God. Let us have brotherhood, but not by all means." Dean Pope was also critical of the "peace of mind cult." "It is not likely that a few psychological gimmicks or changes of attitude will resolve tensions that are really significant. . . . In their effort to be appealing, they quickly become appalling from the standpoint of sincere and well-founded and full-ranging Christian faith" (*New York Times*, March 2, 1955, p. 25, col. 1).

In a moving paragraph on prayer Harry Emerson Fosdick may or may not have had Dr. Norman Vincent Peale in mind. At all events, Dr. Peale could profit by Fosdick's teaching. Cf. Leon and Elfrieda McCauley, eds., *The Book of Prayers* (New York: Dell, 1954), Introduction by Harry Emerson Fosdick, "The Strength of Personal Prayer," p. 10: "To be sure, there are misuses of

With less sparkle but with sobriety and solidity the former editor of the *Christian Century,* Paul Hutchinson, proposed his criticism of Dr. Peale's message in *Life* (38, no. 18 [April 11, 1955] 138–158). Many a Protestant theologian would urge us to overlook Dr. Peale by observing that Dr. Peale's dubious theology is unimportant.

But Dr. Peale is important. In February, 1958, the bookstores were selling copies of the nineteenth printing of the work, which first appeared in October, 1952. By May, 1955, over a million copies were sold. Millions have read the book, even though it has not yet been published in the pocket-book market. More millions have read the serialized publication in the Hearst papers. In addition Dr. Peale has a numerous radio and television following; his weekly syndicated column appears in many papers; he conducts a question-and-answer department in the pictorial fortnightly, *Look;* his magazine, *Guideposts,* his sermons and his tracts engage exclusively a publishing house established for this purpose; the *Reader's Digest* with its millions of readers gives him space. Dr. Peale, America's "Minister to the Millions," is important because he is highly significant as a barometer for contemporary Protestant religiosity.

What is Peale's theory of Christianity? *The Power of*

---

prayer, and many souls have been estranged from praying and deprived of its consolations and reinforcements because they have seen so much superstition and self-seeking mingled with it. Prayer is not a magic way of getting things without fulfilling the conditions of getting them. Prayer is not a process by which mortal man turns eternal God into a bell-boy to run his errands. Prayer is not an emergency measure by which men who otherwise seldom think of God get themselves out of tight places. Prayer is not an ivory tower, a place of soft retreat, to which cowardly souls merely run away to escape from life. Such misuses of prayer are its perversions and caricatures. In the genuine Christian heritage, God, to those who knew the deep meanings of prayer, has been an unseen Friend, an invisible Companion. When they were alone, they were never alone. Then, when emergency came, they traveled an accustomed road, like Jesus in Gethsemane, to a familiar Presence for a brief colloquy, to emerge again ready to face the wrath of devils and the scorn of men."

Positive Thinking claims to be practical and consequently does not really wish to answer that question. Reading the book with concentration—a difficult thing to do—reveals some ideas, but there is no explicitly theological doctrine presented in the work. The only theological message conveyed by the book is through a produced impression that theology is quite unimportant and irrelevant to the real value of Christianity. The type of scholarship involved in the volume can perhaps be illustrated by the author's little excursus into philology, where we are told that "pastor" derives from a word meaning "cure of souls." [27] The ancient phrase, *cura animarum,* is blithely interpreted as soul-healing! This free and easy approach to etymology is paralleled by Dr. Peale's slick use of Scripture quotations. Acts 17:28 is a Pauline borrowing of a phrase from the pagan poet, Epimenides. The text offers an exegete a double problem: (1) What is the meaning of the words in the mind of the original author, Epimenides? (2) How does Paul understand them in the light of his own theology? These questions cannot be easily satisfied. But Dr. Peale has no difficulty at all. He tells us: "In another statement the Bible describes the energizing and re-energizing process: '. . . in Him we live (that is, have vitality), and move (have dynamic energy), and have our being (attain completeness).' " [28] Being of the American Protestant tradition, Dr. Peale offers us quotes from the 23rd (Vulgate 22nd) Psalm on all occasions. It means anything Dr. Peale wants it to mean. There is no need for Dr. Peale to go to the original Hebrew; for any English version is good enough for him, provided the words of the rendition can be used as apparent supports of Dr. Peale's happy message.

Just what does Christianity look like in the light of Dr.

[27] *Power of Positive Thinking,* p. 174.
[28] *Ibid.,* p. 36.

Peale's journalized gospel? It begins beyond doubt with a thorough belief in God. God is omnipotent, loving, and omnipresent. Whether God is a person or merely described by personal symbols is not at all clear. The mere use of personal pronouns when referring to God is no proof that the deity is personal. Certainly God is energy and power. In fact, that truth is about all we need to know. Man is surrounded by a boundless, benevolent energy which he can draw on for the realization of his dreams. I do not wish to be flippant, but it seems that Dr. Peale has reduced God to the status of an unlimited stockpile of free atomic energy. "Take three deep breaths—in and out slowly. Practice resting yourself in God. Practice depending on Him for His support and power. Believe He is giving it to you now and don't get out of touch with that power. Yield yourself to it—let it flow through you." [29]

The great importance given to God in Peale's thought does not prevent his religion from being humanistic. God is something of which man can naturally avail himself. He is a public utility and Dr. Peale merely calls man's attention to its presence and urges the weary soul to make use of it.

This, according to Dr. Peale, is the true and essential message of the Bible—whose content is transparently clear in the old American Standard version. And who is Jesus the Christ? A wonderful, wise man. It is neither affirmed nor denied anywhere that He is God, but He is depicted always as thoroughly human, and the impression is created that He is nothing else. Nor does He play an important part in Peale's message.

What is more, Jesus did just what Dr. Peale is doing—manifesting the enriching power of faith. In fact, not only Christ taught this but men whose belief in God was nil, or at best hazy. Thus Thomas Edison, Ben Franklin, Thomas

[29] *Ibid.*, p. 264.

Jefferson, Ralph W. Emerson and Henry Thoreau are cited
as witnesses to the religious message of Dr. Peale. (I was
looking for a quote from Bob Ingersoll but I do not recall
ever having found it.) Their witness does not seem to be
much inferior to that of Jesus Christ. Dr. Peale says explicitly: "Every such person seems in harmony with nature
and in contact with the Divine energy. They have not necessarily been pious people, but invariably they have been ex-
traordinarily well organized from an emotional and psychological point of view." [30]

It logically follows that Christianity is a practical scheme
for the successful utilization of the powers of nature. We
need not be surprised to hear that it really is a natural
science.

> Christianity may also be thought of as a science. It is a philos-
> ophy, a system of theology, a system of metaphysics, and a sys-
> tem of worship. It also works itself out in moral and ethical
> codes. But Christianity also has the characteristics of a science
> in that it is based upon a book which contains a system of tech-
> niques and formulas designed for the understanding and treat-
> ment of human nature. The laws are so precise and have been
> so often demonstrated when proper conditions of understanding,
> belief, and practice are applied that religion may be said to form
> an exact science.[31]

> The Christianity utilized in this procedure is the undiluted
> teachings of Jesus Christ, Lord and Saviour of man's life. . . .
> Believe [in Christ]; believe in His system of thought and prac-
> tice; believe and you will overcome all fear, hate, inferiority,
> guilt and every form and manner of defeat.[32]

Peale's Christianity pretends to realize the limitless potential in man. There is no room for the doctrine of original
sin, which in the classical Christian vision effectively con-

[30] *Ibid.,* p. 39.
[31] *Ibid.,* p. 220.
[32] *Ibid.,* p. 221.

stricts the human potential for good and renders it incapable of achieving happiness for humanity. If man is to achieve happiness, it will be freely given to him by God working supernaturally and not naturally. This is the doctrine, in one form or other, of all the Christian traditions from the time of the Gospels to the days of Barth and Niebuhr. This continuous tradition Dr. Peale ignores, and if he attaches any meaning to the term, "original sin," he would mean by it an unawareness of the true method of exploiting our natural powers. This unawareness will be overcome by reading the "techniques," "formulas," "principles," "scientific suggestions" of the Bible according to Dr. Norman Vincent Peale.

Paul preached Christ and Him crucified. Peale preaches Christ successful like the innumerable business executives, well known actors, popular football coaches, and radio impressarios who figure on almost every page of Dr. Peale's book. St. John of the Cross spoke movingly of the Dark Night of the Soul. Unfortunately for him, he never had the chance of reading Dr. Peale, who would have explained to him that by positive thinking he could have blown the darkness away.

Is there anything left of the Christian message as either the Protestant or Catholic traditions conserve it? Well, there is a belief in immortality. However, it is not conceived as a heaven-or-hell situation. Speaking of the dead, Dr. Peale says: "Where are they? What is their condition? What sort of body have they? These are questions that are difficult. The idea of a different dimension is probably the most tenable, or it may be more accurate to believe that they live in a different frequency cycle." [33] How did Dr. Peale come to this incredible belief in immortality?

These convictions are based upon sound foundations, the Bible for one. I believe that the Bible gives us a very subtle, and as

[33] *Ibid.*, pp. 253-254.

will be proved ultimately, a scientific series of insights into the great question, "What happens when a man leaves this world?" Also the Bible very wisely tells us that we know these truths by faith. Henri Bergson, the philosopher, says the surest way to truth is by perception, by intuition, by reasoning to a certain point, then by taking a "mortal leap," and by intuition attaining the truth. You come to some glorious moment where you simply "know." That is the way it happened to me.[34]

Neglecting all comment concerning this astounding epistemology, we can yet see that Dr. Peale is not a Biblical literalist. The Bible gives him only subtle hints and "scientific" insights. On the basis of such acquisitions he builds his Christian vision. By this method he can easily pass over the words "sin," "self-renunciation," "suffering," "hell," "punishment," and "the scandal of the cross."

However, he still retains prayer and makes very much of it. But this is "scientific prayer." [35] It has nothing to do with mystical contemplation, but it is wonderful just the same. In its essence it is a verbalized recollection of the limitless energy at our disposal; it is the consoling recognition of the benevolent force which surrounds and sustains us. Its function is therapeutic and it works by itself. Nowhere is it mentioned that God may not answer the prayer, or that the key to successful prayer is found in the phrase, "Thy will be done, not mine." Though Dr. Peale does not say so, the psychologists would say that Peale's prayer is an immense effort at autosuggestion. The psychologists warn their readers that autosuggestion has limits of applicability, but Dr. Peale gives us no warnings. Pray and you will be able to achieve your ambitions, or perhaps even something better. Just pray and you will be spontaneously soothed and you will feel yourself drawing on the omnipresent, infinite energy which is called God.

[34] *Ibid.*, p. 249.
[35] *Ibid.*, pp. 53, 174.

Such is Dr. Peale's conception of Christianity. It has little of the Christianity taught by the Gospels and St. Paul, by Augustine and Aquinas, by Luther and Calvin. Where elements of traditional Christianity are retained, they are given a twist so that they emerge in a guise utterly alien to the sources. Dr. Peale's doctrine, in as far as any theory is involved, is a bubbling *mélange* of Ralph Waldo Emerson, Mary Baker Eddy, and Dr. Emile Coué. We need not lose our temper at the sight of this witch's broth, but we have the right and duty to protest bitterly when it is labeled as Christianity.

The thought content of Dr. Peale's message is anemically thin. Moreover, his mode of expression is not wholly worthy. A dignity belongs to the religious message, because it deals with God, to whom the least we owe is reverence. Just because the stylized pomposity of the older preachers is *démodé,* we are not justified in approaching perilously close to the tawdry. The Negro spirituals are not pompous but their dignity is palpable. Dr. Peale, on the other hand, exploits to the utmost the unesthetic jargon of commercial advertising. When, speaking of prayer, he tells us: "The formula is: (1) PRAYERIZE, (2) PICTURIZE, (3) ACTUALIZE," [36] one does not think of the numinous but of an electric shaver.

It is also of questionable taste to load the text with testimonial letters in the form of quotations from Frank Hiller, the baseball pitcher; Knute Rockne, the football coach; Arthur Godfrey, the radio entertainer; Thomas Edison, the unbeliever; Grove Patterson, editor of the Toledo *Blade;* Hugh Fullerton, the sports writer, and a host of other popular worthies. Nor is the reader edified by repeated "plugs" for other Peale publications and for the Marble Collegiate Church (which is more often identified by city, street, and

[36] *Ibid.,* p. 55.

number). [37] Perhaps the most annoying trick of all is the fawning use of the word, "scientific." Science in our day is revered, respected and exalted. Dr. Peale wants these qualities for his message, and so he simply calls his message scientific. This is utterly misleading. There is no science in Dr. Peale's gospel, and it would be candid to say so simply. If the theologians long erred by attempting to subject science to theology, it is yet a greater error to subsume religion under science.

The reader of Dr. Peale's book cannot possibly avoid the impression that he is listening to a pitchman, who uses every form of mass appeal to induce his hearers to acquire his wares. This is not the climate in which religious truth is either taught or learned.

In conclusion the Catholic voices his concern. It is well known that in the past the Protestant faithful were not deeply influenced by the destructive speculations of the historicist theologians of the nineteenth century. Moralistic naturalism flourished in the universities and orthodoxy was at home in the churches. Today, however, there is more orthodoxy in the universities than in the churches. Missouri Synod Lutherans and fundamentalists still strive to conserve the faith delivered to the saints, but the other churches have no sense of tradition at all. The air they breathe is reconstructionism. Little by little the whole substance of Christianity is being leached out of the churches and nihilism is taking its place. God is anything you accept as absolute; Christ is an ideal construct suggested by the man Jesus; the sacraments are ethical symbols; the Bible contains only moving insights. A

---

[37] On p. 210 Dr. Peale protests that he does not cite his magazine in order to advertise it, although he admits that he strongly recommends it because of the good it can do.

Hindu can accept this and so can an atheist. You can call them Christians, if you wish, and perhaps they would not mind. However, in the whole course of Christianity the Christians did not believe that this was possible. They felt themselves to be a chosen people, set apart through their acceptation of the revelation of Jesus Christ, our Lord, God and Saviour.

"And Elijah came near to all the people, and said: 'How long will you go limping with two different opinions? If the Lord is God, follow him; but if Baal, then follow him.'" (I Kings 18:21.)

9

✢✢✢

Ecumenism and the Catholic

✢✢✢

MANY WRITERS have judged that the phenomenon most conspicuous at this point of the evolution of Christianity is the ecumenical movement, along with its concrete expression in the World Council of Churches. The Evanston meeting of the Council in August of 1954 brought this phenomenon palpably to the American scene. The Council is something definitely new. It offers something to the future, although it would be hazardous to say just what the future will accept. In the evolution of Christianity through the ages, the World Council is an impressive point of departure, no matter what its final fate may be.

The constituent churches, 170 in round numbers, represent every geographical division of the globe. The churches of the Far East are not only members but very vocal along lines not only unusual but at times even embarrassing for the West. No large Protestant denomination is missing, and non-Protestant churches like the Orthodox and Old Catholics add dignity and the appearance of completeness. However, if the large number of churches belonging to the Council impresses, the hole left by the missing churches also attracts attention. The Moscow patriarchate of the Orthodox Church is not a member of the Council, and that patriarchate is probably the most numerous section of contemporary Orthodoxy. Among the Protestant absentees must be mentioned the vibrant "small sects" and the fundamentalist churches in general. Numerically these groups are not very great and usually are smaller than most of the communities in the Council, but they are energetic and highly active in today's world.

However, the startling absence of the Roman Catholic Church has a special significance. In terms of numbers Christianity can be divided into two groups, the Catholic and the non-Catholic, each division comprising roughly 50 per cent of the total. With the Catholics absent, the Council is hardly the voice of Christianity. With the absence of the Russian Orthodox Church, and of the fundamentalist churches, it would be presumptuous to say that the Council manifests the mind of non-Catholic Christianity. According to the logic of things, one must suppose that the supporters of the World Council want the absent churches to come into their union. In consequence, a Catholic should be able to discuss the matter with the adherents of the Council. A dialogue is called for.

First and foremost, the Catholics are not hostile to the ecumenical movement or its fruit, the World Council. On the contrary, they have many motives for wishing the ecumenists well. If we cannot all be one, it is certainly better that we be grouped in two or three units rather than in three hundred. Secondly, from a Catholic's viewpoint, a non-Catholic union can under God's grace be the initial step toward reunion with the Catholic Church. After all, only the Catholic Church can be the logical center of universal reunion. A reunion between Protestants and Catholics, or between Catholics and Orthodox, by the lexicographic tenor of the word, is possible. A reunion between Protestants and Orthodox, strictly speaking, is impossible because those churches were never historically united. Thirdly, the scandal of the divisions of shattered Christianity pains the Catholic no less but even more than it does the non-Catholic. If this division can be only slightly healed, the scandal becomes less painful. Lastly, and in importance firstly, Christian charity drives toward union, and the greater union of Christians, even though highly imperfect, rejoices the Catholic heart motivated by charity. Confrontation is possible only when there is union within the confronting camps.

If all this is true, why then is the Catholic Church outside the ecumenical movement? To this question we must promptly reply that the supposition of the question is not verified. There are at least four conspicuous groups within Catholicism working for ecumenical union. There is the Catholic Oecumenical Conference under the stimulating secretaryship of Dr. J. Willebrands of Holland. This organization meets yearly with delegates from all over the world. In its 1953 meeting at Dijnselburg, Holland, as well as in its 1954 meeting at Mainz, the group discussed the identical themes of the 1954 Evanston meeting of the World Council. In the German-speaking lands, under the patronage of the Bishop of Paderborn, ably seconded by men like Dr. Robert Grosche of Cologne, there is a group at work. In Germany likewise we find the Una Sancta group, founded by the martyr-priest Father Max Josef Metzger (d. 1944), with Catholic and non-Catholic members. With headquarters in Rome the Unitas association, led by Charles Boyer, S.J., is exclusively ecumenist in its work.

In this country the Unitas movement is carried on by the Friars of the Atonement (At-one-ment), a Franciscan group founded primarily for the work of reunion. Another religious family dedicated from its origins to ecumenism is the Chevetogne Priory of the Benedictines in Belgium. The Assumpionist Fathers all over the world are ecumenically active.

The Chevetogne monks are best known for their ecumenical periodical, *Irenikon*. The Unitas group publishes its own organ, *Unitas,* in several languages. Another ecumenical review of distinction is *Istina* directed by the French Dominican, Rev. P. J. Dumont of Paris. Dom Thomas Sartory, O.S.B., edits *Una Sancta* as an organ for that movement, and it is published by the Kyrios Verlag of Meitingen. Herder's *Korrespondenz* from Freiburg i. Breisgau is not exclusively given over to ecumenical work but it is highly sympathetic with such enterprises, as many of its articles show. Primarily interested in reunion with the Eastern Churches, Dom Bede Winslow, O.S.B. and Donald Attwater publish their *Eastern Churches Quarterly* from England.

However, the prevailing interest today is not so much in ecumenical movements as in *the* ecumenical movement concretely expressed in the World Council of Churches, and in this organization the Catholic Church has refused to take part. This is obviously true, but it is also true, as one of the conspicuous figures in the World Council, Father George Florovsky, Professor of the Harvard School of Divinity, has pointed out,[1] that the Catholics are very much interested in the World Council and they are in general sympathetic with it.

Once again one can ask, If this be so, why are the Catholics so conspicuously absent from the organization? With a smirk someone might answer that it is because of a prohibition of the Roman authorities. This is certainly true, but from its nature it is not the ultimate answer. The real question is, What is the basis of the Roman prohibition?

---

[1] Rt. Rev. George Florovsky, D.D., "The Orthodox Church and the World Council of Churches," *St. Vladimir's Seminary Quarterly* (New York), II, No. 4 (Summer, 1954), 14.

The Roman legislation itself meets with different reactions even among Catholics. There are those who have little patience with non-Catholics, for they consider them all as either fools or knaves. Men and women of this mind will enthusiastically applaud the Roman directive and they will do everything possible to see that the legislation is strictly enforced. There are others not quite so militant but thoroughly in favor of the prohibition. These are anxious to communicate with non-Catholics in order to bring them to the Church. However, in order to achieve their aims they limit themselves to the erection of an ever more imposing, more coherent, more flourishing Catholic Church. They restrict themselves, in their approach to the non-Catholic, to the medium of the palpable success of Catholicism as an organization visible to all. Such Catholics have no desire to enter into a verbal dialogue with non-Catholics nor are they eager to meet them halfway. They only point triumphantly to the handsome door, wide open, of their church. It is now up to the non-Catholic. If he wishes to enter, splendid; he is welcome. If he does not wish to enter, he is in bad faith and he had better be avoided.

On the other side of the spectrum stand those Catholics who are so anxious to have the non-Catholics come into the Church that they are willing, if not to compromise with Catholic doctrine, at least to slur over canonized formulas in order to let the non-Catholic come into the Church almost on his own terms. Such Catholics will be annoyed by the Roman restrictions and there is engendered in them a subtle anti-Roman attitude, though nothing would be further from their minds than the denial, explicit or implicit, of Roman primacy and universal Roman jurisdiction.

Between these extreme positions we have countless Catholics, theologians and nontheologians, who are aware of the apostolic nature of Catholicism and they feel the urge of charity pushing them on to an encounter with non-Catholics.

They feel that they must meet the non-Catholics person to person in love and friendship, for only in this climate can an effective conversation be held. There is no desire to make proselytes after the manner of a political party which wishes to aggrandize itself through numerical increase. Rather there is an altruistic wish to have non-Catholics share in the riches of the Church's dispensation of grace. Under this pressure the Catholic is impelled to look toward the World Council where a loving fellowship seems to exist. However, on looking closer he is soon halted because of spontaneous reflections —which are the ultimate basis of the Roman prohibition against participation. A closer view of the World Council raises serious doubts whether the Council is the proper place in which to meet the non-Catholic honestly, courteously and to his advantage.

The World Council, like everything else in history, is conditioned by the original and contemporary environments which are the settings of its being and of which it is a function. Bishop Charles Brent (1862–1929), the Protestant Episcopal father of the Faith and Order movement which helped to produce the World Council, was stimulated to work for ecumenism because as a missionary bishop in the Philippines he was scandalized by the phenomenon of Christianity passionately divided with hideous visibility in the Orient. Hostility, mistrust, needless reduplication of effort, and confusion were the fruits of such schism. He energetically desired to end all this, and he hoped that the Catholics might see a way in which they could join him in his work.

Since Bishop Brent's day Protestantism has passed through a grave crisis. In the words of the brilliant theologian, Paul Tillich, formerly of the Union Theological Seminary of New York and now at Harvard, the Protestant era has ended. The Protestant churches in the thirties woke up to find that their peculiar world vision was no longer important in the total life of the West, and that Catholicism was strongly influencing lands which were supposed to be Protestant *ohne Sagen*. The Catholics of Holland are now on the eve of becoming the majority of a land once staunchly Protestant. In Western Germany, the Catholics are only slightly less than 50 per cent of the Republic, and actually more influential than the Protestants. In the United States the Catholics have not grown much percentage-wise. They are still less than a fifth of the nation, but their consolidation is stronger and their efficiency renders them a greater force than their numbers warrant. Something of the same nature is occurring in Great Britain. If the numerical growth of the Catholics is not too startling, the growing prestige and power which they wield are certainly thought-provoking.

Moreover, a more serious rival than Catholicism has weakened Protestant influence. Since 1914 the vision whereby the West lives is secularistic and naturalistic. Religion, though not attacked west of the Iron Curtain, is nowhere decisive in the direction of communal affairs. In once stanchly Protestant communities, the Protestant churches have suddenly found themselves relegated to the periphery of things. It is true that the churches have all grown slightly in membership, but they have all lost substantially in their hold on the total community.

The alarm occasioned by these facts has driven the Protestants to plug up anxiously the leaks through which their strength is flowing away. The biggest leak was the splintered multiplicity of churches. The reduction of this multiplicity to some amorphous kind of unity is the World Council. Hence to many a Catholic the World Council is nothing more than "Protestantism, Inc.," in spite of the presence of some Orthodox churches and the absence of such genuinely Protestant groups as the "smaller sects" and the fundamentalists.

Friends and champions of the World Council constantly warn everybody that the unity they have achieved is not too strong. It is not one church but a confederation of churches. The very concept of church, except in its most obvious sense, is a source of division in the Council. An Orthodox delegate at Evanston was struck deeply by the failure of the meeting to recognize the implicit ecclesiological dimensions of their propositions and messages. In consequence the Evanston meeting ended in a moving and contrite confession of the sinning Church. The Orthodox in strict logic were obliged to make a courteous protest. For Orthodox and Catholic, the Church is one, holy and visible. A holy church by definition does not sin, even though many of its members, high and low, be grievous sinners who by that very fact reduce the vital activity of the Mystical Body of Christ. To Catholics and Orthodox this is obvious and elemental. To the Protestant, so far from being obvious, such doctrine is unchristian and idolatrous. The Evanston message makes sense only on the postulates of Protestant ecclesiologies, for all Protestants, and even the Anglo-Catholics with some reservations, will willingly, if not insistently, admit that the visible church or churches as such are guilty of sin. They admit perhaps that the invisible Church is sinless, but this admission is possible because the invisible Church is the unrealizable ideal of the churches, or a mystical union unconsciously formed by the sinless saints.

Unless he be present merely as an informal observer, clearly tagged as such, the Catholic would be in an utterly false position in a meeting of a fellowship which rests on such ideas. If he were a formal member of the meeting, he would unavoidably give the impression that he somehow subscribes to such ecclesiologies, or at least considers them valid starting points in the effort to bring the churches into the unity of the *Una Sancta*. Now this is what the Catholic can never do. For him the *Una Sancta* is here already; she needs not to be constructed and, because of the divine structure in her, she cannot be reconstructed without becoming something else. Even though she is human, and thus within history and all its ambiguities, she cannot be substantially corrupted. Since her appearance at the great Pentecostal manifestation of the Spirit, she has never disappeared nor will she ever disappear, and only in her are the means of salvation. For a man of such beliefs it would be a torturing experience to be actively present in a religious fellowship where the operating postulates of the vast majority convict such belief as archaic nonsense or arrogant blasphemy. If he has to speak to the group, he will be misunderstood no matter what he says.

It may be objected that this is all pure apriorism. The fact is that the Orthodox hold the same doctrine as the Catholics in this matter, and the Orthodox feel themselves welcome and at ease. This can be quite true, though many an Orthodox is not too comfortable in his adhesion to the World Council. His best justification for his presence is that it gives him an opportunity to render effective witness to the Orthodox doctrine, which alone is true. This apologetic for the Orthodox participation in Council meetings has its merit but, if it is valid at all, it is valid only for the Orthodox, not for the Catholics. The Protestants, who as the overwhelming majority of the Council will create its atmosphere, are not prone to be offended by the stands and positions of the Orthodox whose thought and work do not impinge directly or deeply on Protestant existence. Precisely because of this fact it can be questioned whether the Orthodox can seriously affect the thinking of the World Council. Might not a cynic say that the Council will give the Orthodox every consideration because their presence offsets the absence of the Catholics with whom the final confrontation must come?

If the Catholic were officially and actively participating

in the Council, his position would be quite different from that of the Orthodox. The Catholic historically is the antagonist who looms large in Protestant fears and dislikes. For so many Protestants he is the wolf at the door. It is easy to get angry with him. Was not some of this anger manifested unconsciously at Evanston in the asperity which dripped from the speeches against the dubiously significant persecution of Protestant evangelists in South America and Spain? Many a Catholic, perhaps not altogether without reason, believes that if you scratch a Protestant, you will find an anti-Catholic. To such a man, entry into the World Council would be tantamount to entering the lions' den. Under such circumstances an irenic conversation seems out of the question.

A non-Catholic's reaction to these guileless observations will be one of exasperation. He will resent being told that the Protestant attitude makes an official Catholic-Protestant dialogue not only difficult but even impossible. The Protestant is deeply convinced that the shoe is on the other foot. He finds that his own position is humble and reasonable, for he is willing to make concessions and he expects the Catholics to do the same. He knows that there are serious differences between the Catholic and Protestant faiths, and he is handsomely willing to come with an open mind to the analysis of these differences, and if need be he is ready to split the differences in a gentlemanly fashion. But he sees that the Catholics have no such intention. They demand that he give up everything which is peculiar and essential to his specifically Protestant position. This he finds uncharitable, unreasonable and intransigent, with the result that he is filled with irritation and impatience.

Yet without realizing it the Protestant spontaneously and in good faith demands that the Catholic, with whom he wishes to discuss, give up his Catholicism while he, the

Protestant, can go on being Protestant. It is true that the
Catholic in his turn asks the Protestant to cease being Protestant as the price of reunion, but the Catholic knows and
admits that this is his demand. The Protestant is not even
aware that his position is identical and just as intransigent.

The Protestant comes to the conversation supposing that
both sides in the historical conflict have made serious mistakes. So far the Catholic can go along with him. However,
the Protestant supposes that these mistakes were on every
level, including the level of doctrine and revealed dogma.
He is willing to bring the old controverted issues into the
light of day, to judge them in good faith, or declare them
irrelevant to modern concern. He is willing to do this in
irenic collaboration with his Catholic brother. However, his
willingness implicitly proclaims his right to judge the Catholic Church even in the field of dogma. This was the position
of the original reformers and it must be ever the position of
any Protestant who really deserves the name. As a true Protestant he cannot accept anything which has not been passed *in
atomo* before the bar of his own judgment. By this principle
he makes himself inevitably the judge of the Catholic
Church, and hence he is put over and above her. For a
Catholic this is *hybris* and blasphemous presumption. The
Catholic insists that man dare not judge God and His word,
and the word of God is spoken by the Catholic Church only,
for the divinely inspired Scriptures and the ecclesiastical
tradition are merely two means whereby the Church infalli-
bly communicates her message. The moment a Catholic
drops this point of view, he automatically ceases to be a
Catholic. He implicitly drops his conviction when he is willing to drop any proposition taught by the Church as the
genuine word of God, or if he seriously enters into a conversation where the silently operating postulate is such a
willingness.

When this is clearly recognized by both parties, it seems that neither Catholic nor Protestant could want the Catholic Church as a member of the World Council of Churches. The Protestant need only reflect that the Catholics could not take seriously the rationale of World Council debates which are organized to construct or reconstruct, eliminate or adapt, or merely criticize the traditional dogmas. On such a reflection the Protestant would be the first to keep the Catholic Church out of his Council. Nor is there an analogy between Orthodox and Catholics on this point. The Orthodox achieve dogmatic definitions by so slow and vague an evolution that much freedom is given to the Orthodox theologians for their opinions. The only form of definition possible in the Orthodox churches is clear consensus, and this is obtained in a very small area, an area already explored by the first seven councils. The position of Catholics is clearly otherwise.

If the Protestant should not want the Catholic in his Council, it is even more true that the Catholic should not wish to be a member. He cannot accept in logic the basic premise of the Council meetings whereby men judge the Church. This may explain more profoundly the lack of interest of the generality of Catholics in the question of membership in the Council. So many see in the new ecumenism another instance of the reluctant return of Protestantism to essential elements of Christianity which, like ecclesiology, sacraments and liturgy, were originally rejected as popery.

It seems that the Orthodox do not substantially disagree with this position. The instruction of the Ecumenical Patriarch Athenagoras to his delegate for the Lund meeting of the Faith and Order committee of the Council in 1952 seems to make the Orthodox adherence a reserved one. The Patriarch admonished the delegate not to enter into discussion concerning the reconstruction or elimination of dogmas, nor to take part in their criticism. The delegate was to do no more than give witness to the perennial tradition of the Church. The other Orthodox churches are not bound to obey the Ecumenical Patriarch, but the fact that they framed a protest against the Evanston message in the name of the traditional doctrine of Orthodoxy indicates that the Patriarch's conception of Orthodox activity at the Council meetings is also shared by them. What would the Orthodox do if the World Council were constituted principally by the Nestorians, Jacobites, Copts and Ethiopians? It is not too rash to presume that they would keep away from the meetings.

But could not the Catholics imitate the Orthodox at least to the degree of being official but passive observers? It seems to me that this question should be answered with some distinctions. Individual Catholics officially representing secular or religious journals have always attended the meetings. Even at Evanston where the prohibition against Catholic participation was very strict, Catholics covered the meetings for the press.

There seems to be no difficulty even in a more intimate participation by the informal attendance of Catholic ecumenists as representative of Catholic ecumenist associations or reviews. This has been done and it is not at all apparent that this involves any inconsistency with our commitments. However, since existential factors enter into the picture, the propriety of such presence would have to be judged concretely by the local bishop who will consult the Roman mind. What is more, at Lund the Catholic bishop in whose area of Catholic jurisdiction the meeting was taking place sent personal representatives in answer to the personal invitation to attend the sessions as a guest. Nothing official was involved and the bishop acted on previous consultation with Rome.

But the Catholic Church, either local or ecumenical, cannot in charity and courtesy send a formal delegate. Such a man would be a misfit in the Council meetings, for his presence would be a silent protest to all that was going on. Protestors from beyond the circle of a union are impolite intruders into the meetings of the union, even if they have tickets of admittance. It is only a rude guest who criticizes the arrangements and ideas of his host, even if his criticism is merely tacit. A formal Catholic delegate would be an official alien critic of the sessions, and such a concept is logically weird.

Hence from every point of view we see that courtesy and charity demand that the Catholic Church in her formal reality remain absent from Council affiliations and meetings. Her presence can only annoy and molest the true masters of the house. The Catholic Church should not be formally invited to membership, real or honorary, for this unwittingly insults her and, if such an invitation were extended, she should not accept it lest she insult the members of the Council. Charity and courtesy in the ecumenists should urge them to inform the Church of their meeting and projects, and the Church impelled by charity should follow closely and sympathetically what goes on in the Council. Nothing more can be done in love and logic.

Is it then the poor conclusion of this study to state that charity itself forbids the meeting of Catholic with non-Catholic? Hardly that. This study wishes only to point out that the World Council is not the formal place for such an encounter. We must meet elsewhere. There is no question of founding a different kind of Council for, as long as it is a fellowship of churches, we shall have all the inconveniences noted above. The Catholic in logic cannot enter into a union of churches, because the very foundation of Catholicism is the dogma that there is only one Church, and that the word "churches" can have meaning only in the sense that they are local subdivisions of that unique, divine, visible Catholic institution. If there is no God but Allah, it is also true from the Catholic view that there is no church except the Catholic Church.

Have the ecumenists ever thought of the hypothesis of the presence of the Catholic Church in the World Council with a voting power proportionate to her numbers? The Catholic Church would then outvote all the others, and they would in conscience be obliged to leave their own Council!

Yet Catholics and non-Catholics can meet in harmony, as long as the meetings are unofficial. The Una Sancta movement in German lands may not be as strong as it once was, but it shows what can be done along these lines. Catholic and Lutheran theologians meet periodically to discuss the problems involved in reunion. The act is not of the Catholic Church nor of the Lutheran Church nor yet of both churches in combination. It is the act of a private group united by the Christian desire for the total union of all Christians. Moreover, the members of the group are equipped with the competence in theology requisite for their undertaking. For neither side is there any inconsistency, and on both sides charity is highly visible.

The German Una Sancta is an organized association. However, formal organization is not necessary for such work. Small groups everywhere, inspired by love of the neighbor and the Church, and equipped with competent theological guidance can produce a climate in which reunion can germinate. The lack of formality would not mean total irresponsibility, for the Catholics would have to work with the cognizance of their bishop. However, they would in no sense be official and consequently they would be freer in their discussions. The smallness of the groups implies no disadvantage, for in small groups there comes a more intimate acquaintance with the group members, which would be an aid to charity that thrives on understanding. Besides, many

small groups widely spread over the world can be more efficient in the production of reunion than one large association
with headquarters far away even for those who live in its
shadow. We must go to the grassroots, for the nearer the
ecumenical movement comes to the soil of the commonality
of believers the greater are its prospects of achieving its high
goal.

This is one Catholic's mind on the manner in which Catholics can meet non-Catholics. Not formally in the meetings of
the World Council, for which Catholics have nonetheless respect and good will. We can meet efficiently and cordially in
many small local groups in which with Christian freedom
and love we can speak our minds and hearts. This is certainly possible. What is more, it is urgent, for we must come
together lest many a soul, cut off from a strong Christian
unity, grow slack and listless and thus become a ready prey
to naturalism or worse. The way proposed is Catholic with
the Catholicism of St. Paul speaking in the shadow of the
many altars of the Acropolis. It is certainly a simple but viable answer to the question of ecumenical dialogue.